A Modern Odyssey

A Modern Odyssey

R. M. Hart

VANTAGE PRESS
New York

FIRST EDITION

All rights reserved, including the right of
reproduction in whole or in part in any form.

Copyright © 1998 by R. M. Hart

Published by Vantage Press, Inc.
516 West 34th Street, New York, New York 10001

Manufactured in the United States of America
ISBN: 0-533-12382-8

Library of Congress Catalog Card No.: 97-90399

0 9 8 7 6 5 4 3 2 1

To Vickie and Bill, my anchors down through the years

Contents

Preface ix

I.	Encounter	1
II.	December 7—The Odyssey Begins	8
III.	Embarkation	11
IV.	The Weaving Begins	13
V.	Planning for the Trojan Horse	16
VI.	The Unraveling Begins	20
VII.	The Trojan Horse Is Readied	22
VIII.	On the Beach	30
IX.	VE Day and Beyond	40
X.	Circe Spins a Web	44
XI.	A New War	47
XII.	The Long Way Back	58
XIII.	The Long Way Home	64

Preface

If men didn't like to engage in battle, one place or another, there would be no wars. From tribes taking up spears and shields and clambering up one side of the mountain or slogging through jungles to fight another tribe, to boxing rings, football fields and golf courses, they still do. The split atom may change all that. World War II and the "police actions" of Korea and Vietnam, plus the *lebensraum* excursions of Russia and other countries in various parts of the world may have heralded the end of noisy, destructive global confrontations. World War III may be the cowardly and puny incursions of terrorists. Even politicians fear the awesome atom. Rocketry, a product of war and its sophistication, understood only by scientists, could either end wars or end the human race. Little men pushing buttons may replace the heroes of song and story, but there is one last odyssey to relate.

In spite of mental and physical hazards and crippling memories, many of the veterans of the twentieth century find their war experiences the high point of their lives. Never again would they rise to the excitement and danger of those battles, the camaraderie, and the emotional highs that civilian life could never equal. They never painted fearsome faces or uttered wild yells to scare their enemies, but they troop back to Omaha and Utah beaches, to Okinawa and Iwo Jima to view the sites of their historical confrontations. Is war in our genes?

Odysseus was king of Ithaca, farther from the Trojan war than any other monarch. For ten years he wandered, strangely, by a most indirect route. He, apparently, for an expert soldier, foolishly exposed himself and his men to ruinous adventures. Circe and the Sirens beset him, perhaps as penance for some of his deeds. Calypso enthralled him for eight years. Penelope, his wife, weaved and unraveled to avoid the suitors who were beseeching her, wrecking her home and wasting Odysseus's resources. Could it be he did not want to return home?

Jack was Plato's soldier incarnate, born to that role. The war was far from America's shores, but it threatened that continent as surely as the Trojan conflict threatened the Adriatic. He fought through Europe and Asia. It was twenty-four years before his Penelope could cease unraveling and finish her weaving. This is the story of his odyssey.

A Modern Odyssey

I
Encounter

It had been a day like any other. The long, wooden floors of the barracks' hospital took a toll on one's feet. Soldiers had to remain hospitalized until they could return to their pyramidal tents and full duty in the troop streets. The hospital was full of overactive, convalescing young men. They were eager for physical activity and very hard to control. A number were from a National Guard cavalry regiment.

Penny, short for Penelope, was a nurse who, impelled by patriotism, had signed up for a one-year enlistment in the army nurse corps a year before Pearl Harbor. She found these soldiers and their medical needs far different from the patients in the large metropolitan medical center where she had trained. There were boards on kegs for desks and one thermometer for three hundred patients. The orderlies were requisitioned from the motor pool and were completely untrained for these duties.

Penny had been riding a chestnut mare on the Central Park bridle paths for several years and was eagerly accepted by the cavalry troops in her unit, for whom their horses were a joy and way of life. The dust of unpaved streets, long, hot marches on horseback in swamps, unfamiliar insects, the food and accidents on the rifle ranges had taken a toll. Some had been hastily inducted although physically and mentally unfit. They had begged to go with their friends for what seemed like a giant game in January 1941. The rules were different from football and baseball, but your regiment was your team, and you weren't about to see the team leave without you.

They lay there hurrying to get well so that they would not be left behind if their outfit moved out or before someone else was assigned their mount.

There were rumors of movement to the European and African wars, but these seemed faraway, romantic conflicts. Some of the boys were waiting for the red tape to untangle in Washington for their medical discharges to move from some in-basket in the War Department to release them to farms and factories in civilian life. Others were anxious to see action of any kind. It was a hectic hospital, where prostitutes mysteriously got through the gates in taxis and had to be routed from the secluded back porches of the wards by harried nurses who felt like mothers or wardens to mountain boys in a big town for the first time. Some even found their clothes and went AWOL if their cousins in the troop street decided they wanted to go home and forget this war or go to a party.

One day, a captain from the cavalry unit came to bring pay to his troops. Penny had only been in camp a few days and felt strange and new. Dressed in a World War I uniform that had been shortened—no Mainbocher then—she felt less than a great beauty and hardly presentable as the boys introduced her to the captain as one from their and her own state who liked to ride and knew horses. He left with little to say and visited some other wards but in ten minutes he was back, inviting her to the officers' mess at his unit. She gladly accepted. It seems banal in the telling, but it was the beginning of a long, heartbreaking saga of love, separation, and loneliness.

Penny had arrived in camp with a pedigreed cocker spaniel puppy she had purchased shortly before deciding to join the army. Recruiters on Governor's Island in New York told her blithely that "nurses are housed in homes, and it will be quite all right to take the dog." She arrived after a long drive south to find an irate peacetime chief nurse, out of her administrative depth, who berated her for such foolishness. Rather than houses for nurses, they were assigned to barracks with little or no privacy and no place or desire for a canine mascot who needed as much attention as a human baby. Several boarding arrangements did not work out and were too expensive for the seventy-dollar-a-month salary given nurses who were officers in name only and received no allowance for quarters or pay comparable to the male officers.

Jack, finding out about the dog problem, offered his blacksmith and shop to care for the pet. Gradually she became the mascot for Troop A and enjoyed daily swims in the concrete horse troughs, kissing the horses' noses as she swam by. Except for the colonel, who didn't know much about horses and didn't understand the special relationship between horses and dogs, she had a blissful existence. Every time he caught her in the trough, he bellowed, "Get that goddamned dog out of there." The boys removed her, but she went right back in as soon as he left, to the delight of the troops who always liked nothing better than to hoodwink their commander, particularly one who was not popular. Me=too, for that was her apt name, disrupted a *gymkhana* for a visiting general one day by getting out of the blacksmith's shop and darting out into the review to greet her favorite horse and its rider, Jack. He had become so fond of her that these exploits did not disturb him, and she frequently slept with him on his narrow army cot in the canvas tent. She also had visits to the troop veterinarian to interrupt several unauthorized pregnancies engendered by various camp followers. These were kept from Penny as too lewd for 1941 sensibilities. The dog, however, had a sixty-three-day pseudopsyesis which alerted Penny to the danger of a pedigreed pup in an army setting.

It was a halcyon few months for Penny and Jack who quickly became lovers in moments snatched from duties and the surveillance of others. Such affairs were frequent. Nurses could not even become engaged at that time. Even if war was undeclared and unwanted, it was in the very air they breathed, and time was in very short supply. There were long horseback rides in the pine woods, pocked with rattlesnake holes and soft Southern nights stolen from needed sleep. Their love nests were rooms or a small apartment where the bed was so covered with bedbugs, they made love on the floor, sleeping there quietly afterwards.

Then came a horrible separation of hundreds of miles, when a small cadre of nurses was sent into the Tennessee hill country to care for Patton's tank corps and other troops on maneuvers as they readied themselves, although unwittingly, for the eventual push that broke the Nazi back. Up in the rolling green hills, miles from anywhere, 70,000 troops descended on the little crossroads town and left it denuded of everything from merchandise to morale. The store shelves were bare. The mud-puddle ponds served as swimming pools if the snakes and alligators were removed first.

The few nurses were besieged. They were the only possible dancing partners for the improvised parties the regiments tried to hold for the tired troops. Penny turned away contentedly from the pleadings. Several officers had tried to date her, but she told them there was someone else in her life, and she had no desire to socialize with anyone else. Her heart was too full of the big, sandy Irishman with the quiet voice and the air of command. In fact, his rank made her disciplining of those troops who knew of their mutual attraction much easier. They did not wish to incur the wrath of his displeasure if they gave her a hard time. She watched and waited for each precious visit. He drove all night to spend a few hours with her, then would hurry back the next day to meet his troops on the rifle ranges, with no rest.

Nothing was too much; no effort too great. It was as if the time pulled them on like a giant magnet and all their actions were willed for them. Although she later burned her pitiful store of letters, she remembered in one of them, "I never understood why the boys went over the hill for a woman, but now I know."

Finally when the maneuver was over, she returned to the sandy coastal plain and so many uncertainties. Rumors were rife. America was slowly edging toward a declaration of war, but Roosevelt was holding back, unwilling to take that giant step into the debacle.

Bombs were falling on Great Britain, and they suffered several defeats at the hands of the Germans. Factories were gearing up for war production. New automobiles were proscribed for civilian use, but Penny had been lucky enough to get one of the last ones available, and so they had transportation for the few times they were able to get away from camp.

In the camp, the tents stretched on sand so hot it burned through the soles of shoes and boots. In the tents lived men with passions and problems. Some were fools and some were very good men; all were caught up in a historical moment far beyond their comprehension. It was just as well. They knew little of the conflict, of the torturous road of European and Asiatic politics that had brought them to this army encampment. They were salesmen, professional men, playboys, and construction workers, far from their accustomed lifestyles and bewildered by it all but playing the game according to some ancient code deep in their genes. The Crusaders must have been impelled by the same drives as they set off on their impossible missions. These men performed the duties of their respective ranks, sometimes well, often badly, sometimes so badly that they were demoted, transferred, or discharged.

There were lighter moments. Jack told Penny, with evident enjoyment, of one prank that happened before she arrived in camp. The troop had a dance for officers and their local dates (in spite of wives back home). When asked who he was bringing, Jack, unmarried and unattached, responded, "Just the prettiest gal there." He was noted for his disinterest in the opposite sex, so rumors were circulating about whom he could possibly be dating.

The night of the dance, all were waiting for an answer; he arrived, riding his dappled dun mare up the ramp and onto the dance floor. Of course the colonel took a really dim view of his "date," and he and Vassar were ordered out before her shoes could mar the rough plank floor.

There was a good deal of politics and currying of favor, both with men and the nurses as well. Penny would never have been promoted, as she could not use some of the tactics she saw others use. She often went outside the chain of command, so dearly loved by the armed services, when she saw some serviceman who needed a discharge or special pass. She was repeatedly warned by the post commander that he would "grant your request this time, but you must go through channels."

Jack, on the other hand, was acutely conscious of the protocols, although he used no methods other than his integrity and ability to achieve promotions. No one could deny that he was an impeccable soldier; his efficiency reports were excellent even though he and the colonel were not fond of each other. He repeatedly enjoyed dreaming up some stunt, which did not endear him to his commanding officer but was much enjoyed by the troops, who came to him for advice and help when needed. He was a soldier's officer.

Some of the officers and men used the absence of wives and families to form new liaisons. Several approached Penny and became angry when she refused to arrange dates for them with nurses from the station hospital. They also did not like the fact that Jack, who had long been close friends with so many of his fellow officers, now spent little time with them. There was so little time, and he spent it all with Penny. Their anger later turned into a vendetta, which may have helped send this latter-day Odysseus on his circuitous route home to Penny.

Through it all, the lovers lived each day involved with their duties and every possible night involved in a passion that in peacetime would have been hard to sustain. Their lovemaking was triggered by the certainty that separation was coming sooner or later and each night might be their last together. Today, so many decades later, it is hard to explain such intensity of feeling.

The final blow, worse even than shipping overseas, came with the order mechanizing the unit. For the men who had lived largely for their mounts and the cavalry tradition, it mattered little that war now moved too swiftly and harshly for horses. Jack's polo ponies would be saddled and mounted by strangers, perhaps at Fort Meyers, and participate only in marches and funerals down Pennsylvania Avenue to Arlington Cemetery.

Vassar tossed her head, her dappled-dun flanks gleaming in the hot sun. Her rider was carefully groomed, his campaign hat with its gold tassels above his stern visage. The troops' appearance was reminiscent of the cavalry charges across the West as the buffalo and Indians vanished under the horses' hoofs. Their tradition had been formed on the Western prairies. Jack had ridden on mounted trips across all of Kansas, from Fort Riley down bluffs and through storms and sun for hundreds of miles. His instructor was General Wainwright, so soon to be captured on Bataan.

It was romance but a sad romance. This was the last parade. The cavalry was now the "mechanized cavalry," complete with jeeps and tanks. Tomorrow, the horses would be loaded in horse trailers that had taken them on so many maneuvers. They were on their way to pasture in Front Royal, Virginia. Strong men wept as they saw their friends for the last time. They had always cared for their mounts before themselves, coming back from the muddy swamps and the coastal plains, even as Marion, the Swamp Fox had done before them in another war. It was a form of selflessness that machines could never equal.

Only half their hearts had been in their year of fighting with bags of flour for bombs, and the enemy a Red or Blue team. Their slogan began to be "Over the Hill in October." The loss of the horses was the last straw. What kind of a war was this anyway?

Their enlistment would be up then, and it would be back home to wives and sweethearts or the new romances they had enjoyed under the hot, Southern sun. But they did not go "over the hill" in October or in November or even in December. On a quiet Sunday in December when they had just returned from an all-night maneuver, a voice with an Eastern prep-school accent told them of an "act which will live in infamy," and their lives and decisions were no longer their own.

II
December 7—The Odyssey Begins

Penny would never forget that day. Every December 7, she was back in that rented apartment on a quiet, back street in that sleepy Southern capital, pecans dropping on the doorstep and a lump of soft coal glowing in the grate. Jack lay on the sofa, tired after the exertions of the last two days, his head in her lap. The outside world was forgotten while soft music came over the small radio. Then that sudden announcement; their world was shattered as surely as by the bombs then falling on Pearl Harbor.

He told her then that he had been expecting this; that as the regiment (G-2), he had been alerted to expect trouble, but the good officer that he was, he had divulged it to no one who did not have a "need to know." How merciful that she had not been able to foresee that day or the miserable ones that would follow. So many of the treasured memories would never have been. Tension would have destroyed their private world.

War is such an immense turmoil, such an all-engulfing dislocation that all else fades into insignificance. Perceptions are heightened, and emotions explode to the surface. Survival, physical and emotional, is all that matters. Even on the North American continent, secure behind its oceans, or so they thought, everything was changed. It was the death of an old world and the beginning of one of which they had no conception. Elemental needs, sights, and sounds fused all into an unforgettable dramatic panorama that left little time or energy to ponder what might come after the fighting ceased. There was no attempt at clear-headed planning; planning for what? For the return to peace? Who knew when this might come or who might be left to greet it? The return to home? Home might have vanished in the dust for all one knew now. For the usual order of things, for courtship, marriage, children, how could one wait? He who lingered and counted costs was lost. Perhaps only memories would remain if one survived the holocaust that flamed overseas.

Penny and Jack had several stolen weekends after war was declared, when they could drive into the surrounding hills, find a motel, and forget for a few hours the impending separation that was sure to come. They climbed Lookout Mountain and stood on a precipice overlooking five states. It was a Civil War campground and battlefield with a plaque to the Alabama regiment who had perched on the mountain shelling the Union forces in another lost cause. By this time, it was certain that shipment overseas was imminent. The only questions were whether it would be Europe, Africa, or the far Pacific theater and when the blow would fall.

They had only a few short months before that fateful day, but it was long enough to realize that some poets were right. It is impossible to love like that again, in the same way, submerged completely in another, feeling alive only in the presence of that love. Heightened by the uncertainties of the wartime situation, each day each hour became dreadfully important.

Even the unpleasant colonel and his watchdog wife recognized something too fragile to destroy and wisely, unusual for them, kept silent in the face of this de facto union. The army, at that time, did not allow its nurses to marry, and many were caught in the same trap. If she remained in the service, she could not marry, and if she left at the end of her enlistment, she would probably be cut off from the few short hours they could spend together. Most of the other service couples treated them with respect and affection. They seemed also to feel something of the need for closeness and love that they might not have felt before such a crisis. They were content not to judge. They banded more closely together to try to protect all that was left of normal life and love, and petty cliques and squabbles were forgotten. Maneuvers and temporary transfers ate pitifully into the remaining hours for officers and enlisted men alike.

III
Embarkation

The summons finally came. It was almost a relief after the unbearable tension of that hot summer. Penny had not reenlisted when her year was up, hoping for marriage, but Jack did not want to be in Europe or Asia leaving behind a wife and possibly a child. She was tearful. He was adamant. It was many years later, after his death, that a cousin told her the real reason for his seeming lack of trust in any woman's fidelity. He had been married when very young and came home to find his wife in bed with another man. He threw the interloper from a second-story window, sash and all, and narrowly missed an assault charge. Jack told her only that he had been briefly married, had never seen his wife again, and did not know if she had ever gotten a divorce. It seemed a poor excuse at the time, but later events and papers she found in his files proved her suspicions were true. He had not lied to her. He did not receive his divorce until after a suitor claimed Penny.

Penny stayed in the area of the military base and worked briefly in a small local hospital. She was offered a permanent position teaching in the segregated nursing school but indignantly rejected the idea that nursing could allow racial barriers. Just about the time that the regiment was to get its orders, her brother's wife died in childbirth, leaving small children. Although she felt very guilty about leaving the service, these proved reason enough to sever her connection with the nurse corps.

Troop movements were blacked out. Penny and the spaniel

made a long lonely trip up the coast, hoping for one last meeting. She searched with several troop wives, accepted as one of them. Finally, they crossed the bay to Staten Island, where they could see the troop ships anchored. There was no way to know which ship their men were on, but they needed to be doing something, anything, until the gray hulks were lost in the fog. The convoy finally left the safe harbor for the submarine-infested open Atlantic.

It was a miserable day followed by many others, as the mails were slow, noncommittal, heavily censored V-mail sheets. Jack's troop was bound for England, another to Africa, and the third to the Pacific. It was indeed a world war. She remained friends with several of the wives, but when Jack's V-mail stopped after a year or so, she was too embarrassed to pry for news.

IV
The Weaving Begins

Penny decided to take a public health position in Jack's home area. She felt if and when he did return to her, that would be the locale in which he would want to live. His relatives and friends were nearby, but because of the tenuous relationship, she did not contact any of them, fearing a rebuff or traumatic rejection. It was a difficult time at best. She even consulted an attorney as to her legal status. This was long before the famous or infamous palimony cases. He informed her, kindly and in an understanding manner, that since the state in which the army post was located allowed common-law marriage, she could claim that. He suggested that she might want to avoid any unpleasantness that such a move would cause, since Jack was unsure of his marital status. His mother received his dependency allotment and was sure to be incensed by any such claim.

Penny had a good position and did not need the allotment, so she decided to stifle her desire for commitment, which could not be substantiated under wartime conditions. She took a good deal of responsibility for her brother's children and twisted the gold troop ring he had given her. She tried to rationalize the future realistically. It looked bleak, but she was so busy between job and children, there was little time to fantasize what might have been. She traveled back and forth from her job and apartment to her brother's home over roads normally filled with thousands of cars, now sometimes completely empty because of gas rationing. Some of her patients had given her extra coupons, since they knew of her situation. In her rare free hours, she knitted, sometimes unraveling what she had made for herself, nieces, and nephews.

Penny was made responsible for the public health of a neighboring town of twenty thousand people. Most were involved with aircraft companies making planes for the military. Their long shifts and good paychecks fortunately kept them healthy and on the job. Her duties, which ordinarily would have been carried out by a physician as health officer, were not too heavy, and she was able to carry them out safely. Penny thought about reenlisting, but her obligations to the job and the children plus some bureaucratic snafus about her serial number made her realize that the home front needed help, too.

There were not many empty hours, but Penny decided to continue her education for a bachelor's degree and traveled several evenings a week to a metropolitan university. She had begun these studies before entering the army and decided to begin premedical courses. She had no idea that medical school would not be a possibility after ten years of nursing experience. She was to learn that gender was an obstacle in the "old boy" mentality of major medical school registrars and faculty. Travel by train was difficult and uncertain. Blackouts were frequent and cut into study time. On occasion, she used fat, white blackout candles and studied far into the night.

At the end of one semester, she faced a final examination in physics. There had been a new instructor every week, to the consternation of the class. No one knew that the physicists were being siphoned off to atomic energy projects around the country. Such secrecy seems impossible in today's world of television news media and "official" leaks, but it was well kept in spite of so many being involved in the bomb's creation. All this kept Penny from spending precious time on worry or self-pity. However, it was at this time that the parade of suitors began. It had been three years, and Penny began to lose hope that there was any future for her unrequited love. Her love never faded, but her self-esteem reached out to other men. She needed admiration.

V
Planning for the Trojan Horse

Although the regiment was no longer intact, several of Jack's long-time friends were still in the now mechanized cavalry. These long-time horsemen carried on the cavalry traditions as a barrier to their dislike of the iron steeds, tanks, that they now rode. They had long resented Jack's involvement with "that nurse." They did not like his defection from the freewheeling days of encampment and local belles. They also resented the fact that Penny had refused to involve her nurse companions in dates that disregarded their wives at home. They may have had some connection with Jack's cavalier treatment of the love he left behind.

They trained hard for the inevitable invasion, but they played hard, too. Jack rode to the hounds over some of England's choicest countryside. They were quartered near Oxford but close enough to sample the nightlife of London. Bombs were falling on that city, but with the sense of fatality common to the born soldier, he did not think one was meant for him or if there was one so marked, there was little he could do about it. Piccadilly Circus swarmed with people. There were soldiers in fifty different uniforms. Refugees from invasion-torn countries arrived to take part in freedom-fighting brigades. There were Norwegians, Dutch in Germanlike uniforms, and young Poles in glamorous uniforms that belied their poor showing in defense of their homeland. Foreign and domestic servicemen were cooped up in tiny England. It was feared they would take that nation apart if they did not get action soon.

Jack was not immune to the war fever and malaise that gripped England. Only a few miles separated these soldiers from their firestorm across the English Channel. Although not a student of history, he had studied campaigns of previous wars. It was obvious to him that this would not be a quick victory, if, indeed, there would be a victory at all. Eleanor Roosevelt visited the troops as her husband's emissary shortly after they arrived on English soil. An arrogant Charles de Gaulle descended on his small, favorite basement restaurant and expected all to rise at his entrance, which, of course, they didn't! Jack wrote less and less and, finally, not at all to his brother or mother, which again, Penny did not learn until many years later. Her self-esteem at rock bottom, she assumed she was the only one he treated so badly. The only news she and probably his family received was from dispatches by a reporter that a local newspaper had sent with the troops. "Major" Jack was frequently mentioned, so the wound was constantly opened.

He had a batman, a necessity for spit-and-polish British officers, but his was a woman, part of the vast pool of British women in the armed services. He never did say if she laid out his clothing, drew his bath, or performed other personal services, which was an inference that could be drawn from reports of other American officers in high places. There was a local joke, "Up with the lark and to bed with the wren."

There was plenty of entertainment for leave days. The Stage Door Canteen opened with the arrival of American troops. Movies were closed when the war first broke out but were reopened when it was obvious that the home front needed a respite from Dunkirk and the ever-present bombing raids. Any place where people congregated, however, was a source of danger. Audiences were warned that they should leave when a raid was imminent and the sirens blew. Plays began at five P.M. so that the audiences could leave before the nightly raids and blackouts. Jack and the Londoners as well were blasé and seldom took cover. He and his pals were drinking in a bar in a converted conservatory with a glass roof when a bomb hit, shattering their watering hole. As usual, he walked away, even as Achilles, without a scratch.

All was not easy for the crowded Britons. They and America had been looking forward to the transatlantic partnership, but a booklet was quickly prepared to brief the G.I.s about language and cultural differences. Americans were warned that they should not brag that they had "come over and won" the last war. Many Britons invited G.I.s to their homes but were warned to ration their drinks and protect their daughters. The black troops were objects of wonder to children and some adults alike. The cockneys said, "Maids were prick-mazed!"

Jack and his friends were wined and dined, and they had access to rooms in the finest hotels, even though lodging was scarce in bomb-pocked London. In spite of drills and briefings, there were plenty of opportunities for fraternization, and they made the most of these. "Waltzing Matilda" and "Over There," and "Lili Marlene," in spite of its German origin, were heard from every street corner, dance hall, cafe, and canteen kitchen. There never was a shortage of girls at Rainbow Corner near Piccadilly Circus. Jack had a horror of venereal disease infection and probably watched some of his colleagues link arms with these willing women but probably abstained himself.

From the autumn Atlantic crossing in 1942, to D-Day in June of 1944, England was a playing field, a prelude to real action, but the desire to fight and get it over with seemed to be basic with all the Allies, British Commonwealth, Norwegians, French, and, of course, the vast American force waiting for the Trojan horse of an armada to be built. The Japanese raids on American shipping in the Pacific created a tremendous logistics problem in supplying the European theater, but those in ranks below the officers in command probably heard little news of why their stay on the island was prolonged.

Jack spent some time in Lord Mountbatten's Scottish castle,

learning to be a commando, to jump from jeeps at forty miles an hour and survival techniques that would stand him in good stead in this and another war. Unlike many of his colleagues, he never complained at these exercises and was cited by Mountbatten himself for his attitude and willingness. Jack was in his glory, loving the drama, the nerve-tingling alertness needed, and his access to all sorts of interesting people, places, and activities.

VI
The Unraveling Begins

The reporter sent back numerous dispatches of the activities of Jack and his fellow officers. Some of them read like a society gossip column, and some indicated that some degree of training was being carried out, though, of course, all were censored. The inept colonel who had been hung in effigy by his troops in the States was still in command, much to the dismay of Jack and some of the other officers who despaired of going into combat with such a leader. Mercifully, he was eventually recalled to the States and was booted upstairs to command all of the National Guard in Washington. The dispatches to the newspaper began to take on a more ominous note as positions were shifted and promotions and demotions made. Jack was made a major and went from squadron commander to battalion commander. He put on an exhibition of reconnaissance activities for British and Allied commanders, which received high praise. All this was duly reported by the correspondent.

Some of the troopers were invalided home, and Penny arranged to meet them for news. They told her that Jack had changed. He was no longer the happy-go-lucky captain they had all followed willingly. "A French divorcee was chasing him around." The period of the suitors began. While she did not have time to knit or unravel, the parallels were there. Penelope must have had the same sense of loss as the years of Odysseus's absence continued.

After several years of no personal contact, Penny gave up hope and foolishly married a naval officer whom she did not really care about, but he lived three thousand miles away and was about to be demobilized. Of course, it was an ill-fated union. Jack had sent his tackle box full of saddles, bridles, and other paraphernalia to her home before they had left camp. She placed the gold ring in an envelope and expressed the box to his mother's home. She felt all ties were broken and left for the West Coast, a continent away from heartbreak. In the West, she subscribed to the newspaper that carried the dispatches. It was obvious that when a love like theirs existed, time and distance could not destroy it, but she did not want to accept this idea.

VII
The Trojan Horse Is Readied

In September 1943, General Bradley had been called away from the British landings on the mainland of Italy across the Straits of Messina. He was disappointed at not being present at this historic event as the Allies finally gained a foothold on the European continent, but he was excited at what seemed to be a new initiative in this interminable war. General Patton, whom he described as both stimulating and overbearing, met him in a gloomy, musty palazzo in Palermo. He informed General Bradley that General Eisenhower, who was then commander-in-chief of the Mediterranean forces, had sent a message that he wished to see General Bradley that day.

At that meeting with General Eisenhower, Bradley was told that the Italians would surrender on September 8. They did not wish German and Allied forces to fight on their sacred Italian soil or further damage their ancient cities and ruins. At that meeting, General Bradley was told that he was to return to England and command an army for the invasion of France.

Jack was present at those meetings. He had been sent to review the reconnaissance activities in the African and Italian landings as a prelude to the hoped-for liberation of France. The Allied command had been feuding over who was to be the supreme commander for this gigantic push, since President Roosevelt, early in 1943, had suggested that the British should supply this person. The Americans were bitter because theirs was the predominant force and their officers were hardened by the African and Italian campaigns. The same disputes must have taken place before the walls of Troy as the various kings and their troops began the final siege. Odysseus might have been the most influential in these meetings; the king who had come the farthest with his troops.

It was finally resolved in this modern war to have Joint Chiefs of Staff, but not without months of wrangling. General Bradley had spearheaded simulated beach landings while in Florida. He felt well-equipped for the sands of Normandy after the gumbo mud of Dog Island in that state. Jack and his men had ridden through the swamps of South Carolina; no sea-water wettings would seem impossible after those rides. One great problem was that his troop had been cannibalized for cadres of good sergeants and junior officers to head companies of raw recruits in the increasing drafts of men Stateside. Jack's troop was composed of tanks for reconnaissance purpose. He was partially satisfied with their combat readiness. He was not as well satisfied with some of the National Guard officers, whose main interests were finding women and alcoholic refreshment during their enforced stay in England.

He subsequently relieved several of them after the Normandy invasion, for which they never forgave him. He was also anathema to the troop blacksmith, who was too old for service when the overseas orders came. His two sons were in the troop, and he wanted to accompany them. They were killed in battle; he never spoke to Jack again, blaming him for their deaths, although what the old man could have done to save them was problematical.

Old loyalties and hometown cliques made command difficult, but he was equal to the task as evidenced and attested to by the letters of commendation and a drawer full of medals as well as the outstanding efficiency reports. Penny did not find these until almost thirty years later, after his death, as she cleaned out files of his odyssey. They reinforced her judgment that this was a most unusual man.

General Bradley returned to England after General Badoglio announced the Italian surrender to the Allies. On his return, "Operation Overlord" was announced. British General Morgan was placed in charge of planning for the invasion. It was concluded that it would be possible in 1944. This left another agonizing wait for Jack and other American soldiers who were chafing for action. Inactivity was never his strong point. By this time, London and the surrounding countryside were not being pounded by the German Luftwaffe. The Home Guard was down-played as the war converged on Europe and Germany. In Germany V-1 and V-2 rocketry was being perfected, but it was not until after the Normandy invasion that a last-gasp effort from the Reich launched those deadly weapons on England. Winston Churchill regretfully disbanded the Home Guard, who, he said, "really knew what democracy meant."

In 1943, Churchill was arguing for more force in Africa and the Mediterranean. General Marshall did not agree but committed an American force to Africa. At the same time the 38th Reconnaissance Battalion was formed. Jack was promoted to lieutenant colonel and was given its command. He was now deeply into the preparations for Operation Overlord, the channel crossing, and the offensive against what was called Fortress Europe. It was small wonder that he, who never was one to commit himself to paper, wrote no one at home.

He did find time to once again mount horseback and ride to the "White Horse Hunt," which was closed to all men. He was invited by the mistress of the hunt. She was an expert horsewoman, not young and definitely not a siren. There was no time or inclination for amorous dalliance. It may have been because he met her when he was jumping horses at Madison Square Garden horse shows in happier times that he had been shown such special favor.

There were others who were singing siren songs, including one woman of dubious background who apparently set her sights on a marriage that would take her to America. This was a much-desired destination of British and other European women, starved for men, food, and clothing. Jack fended off this woman for a time, but more of that later.

Maneuvers, logistics, and planning called for constant attention of upper echelon officers. Those who shirked these duties were quickly weeded out; this was to be the final push, and total commitment was imperative.

It may have once been merry old England, but by the time Overlord was conceived, Jack and his troops were engaged in training for patrol activities in the toughest kind of country. Their mission would be to locate the enemy and advance on hidden machine-gun nests to pave the way for the main army contingents behind them; no one on the home front had any idea of the peril that entailed. When Eisenhower visited Jack's outfit on inspection about a month before the invasion, he told the group's hometown reporter, "You may say I was here, but you may not say what I told my soldiers."

It was a monumental task to build and supply the "horse" that could cross the stormy English Channel. The Germans controlled the Atlantic coast from Narvik in Norway to the Pyrenees of Spain. The U-boat bases were within easy reach of England's sea lanes. England was unable to replace her shipping losses, while Germany fed its armies with manpower, food, and war materials from its captive countries. It seemed an impossible undertaking, but the alternative was too dangerous to ignore. The Japanese destruction of so much naval power at Pearl Harbor almost shocked the United States into abandoning the European problems and the assault on aggressor Germany.

Winston Churchill hastened to Washington to press the need to link the resources of the only two powers left to oppose Hitler. With Overlord, a problem existed to supply enough craft to cross the channel. The European problem was competing with the war in the Pacific, a far-flung operation that required tremendous support. It is hard to realize the intense effort required to fight a world engagement. The stress was harder on those officers who had to make a decision whether or not to overload the craft that were to land troops on the rocky beaches of Normandy. More landing craft were urgently needed. It seems hardly possible that German intelligence did not penetrate the planning of the assault.

Of course, the foot soldiers knew little of the plans for their rendezvous with mortality. There were few opportunities for leaks of information. Military police stood twenty-four-hour duty outside the briefing rooms, which were covered with maps and memoranda. Blackout curtains covered the windows of the ornate, formerly fashionable flats that had been converted to offices for the top planners. In spite of all secrecy, incendiary bombs were dropped nearby, one crashing through the roof of this stronghold of Allied planning. Volunteers swarmed in to put out the fires, but the guard stood his post and was able to safeguard the vital secrets. This one soldier should have been singled out for commendation, since loss or violation of the materials would have resulted in months of delay and compromised the D-Day landings.

A general held a dinner party and lamented some problems to "come after D-Day." His indiscretion caused him to be demoted from major general to colonel, in spite of his West Point background, and he was sent back to the States. Jack was aware of the dangers of loose talk and was no less severe on his staff of junior officers and sergeants.

Fifty-five thousand men were to land on the targeted beaches. Jack and his reconnaissance troops were to be in the first line of assault. No more hazardous duty could have been imagined. He was thankful he had not taken upon himself a wife and a possible family. His credo was that a soldier could not face the multiple uncertainties of overseas combat, separation, and extreme stress and keep his mind on survival for himself and his men. Odysseus must have felt the same at some time during his separation from Penelope.

It is also likely that no combat soldier could realize or stop to think of the stress on the home front, where one could only sit and wait and read the censored dispatches and imagine the worst.

Indeed, the home front was busy fabricating the materials of war and enduring the rationing of food, gasoline, and all sorts of shortages of consumer goods. When Penny told Jack, years later, of the problems of travel under gas rationing, he found it hard to believe, since he always had a jeep filled with gas at his command.

As D-Day approached, General Eisenhower visited various elements of troops who were to go ashore in the first wave of the assault. He visited Jack and his unit. In an impassioned speech, he promised he would "meet them on the beach." He did not keep that promise, though. Southern England was the site of invasion training. The air was electric with the tension of preparedness. Such tension could not be held in check much longer. The whole island that was England throbbed with it. The invasion troops were concentrated in southwest England on the gray moors of Dartmouth and the steep green hills of Cornwall. When General Bradley visited these troops, he tried to allay the gloom and predictions of frightful casualties. He was quoted, although not authorized, that few would not return. Born soldiers, such as Jack, probably realized that these statements were made for morale's sake, but they did reassure the home front, which had little comfort in the dark days of 1943 and 1944.

The little towns and villages were overwhelmed by thousands of American troops. Fathers of pretty, unmarried daughters were hopeful and, indeed, fostered a sort of lend-lease of their own making for an alliance that was stronger than politics could achieve. American soldiers' pay was three times greater than that of the British enlisted men, and American sergeants made more than lower echelon British officers. They spent freely on leave and were well accepted, for the most part, by the British.

Jack was so busy, he had little time or energy for extracurricular activities, but it was during this period that reports filtered back to Penny that Circe was following Jack. This was the breaking point and caused her unwise decision to accept a suitor's proposal of marriage in order to put three thousand miles between herself and the probable return of her unfaithful lover. It was so hard to ascertain the real reason of his lack of communication.

Plans for Overlord continued with some disputes between English and American commanders. After the British disaster at Dunkirk, it was not surprising that they found the invasion possibilities frightening. However, all commanders were warned that any hint of failure would result in that very failure as it filtered down the chain of command to the troops, whose job it was to carry out the invasion. The British and Canadian forces were to taunt the enemy and decoy them away from the American assault beachheads. The ruse worked. Germany expected the assault far up the French coast, far away from where it actually happened. Spreading scarce German manpower along eight hundred miles of Atlantic coastline while beating a disastrous retreat from Russia meant the Allied forces might be able to punch a hole in that defense.

Once the assault troops were briefed on their mission, they were cut off from the rest of England. Civilian traffic in and out of the coastal area was halted. Two thousand intelligence agents were detailed to prevent leaks. In this perimeter, trial assaults were carried out. It is almost inconceivable that the Germans did not penetrate this security, but they did not. They were probably too busy trying to hold their conquests together in the face of mounting disillusion of their own people and their captive countries. All outgoing mail was stopped, so even if Jack had been a letter writer, no one could have heard from him.

The Trojan horse was moved into place on June 5. One general was sent to London to frequent his usual night spots, as his absence might have been noticed. There were many enemy agents in London, but they were purposely handed misinformation. The crafts were assembling at Plymouth. The assault troops were sealed in their cramped boats for several days. They seemed resigned; they dozed, played cards, or even used their assault ramps for diving and swimming platforms. Lines of G.I. khaki laundry hung from Sherman tank antennae.

On June fourth, the channel was rough with five-foot waves. The advance units were called back, complete with seasick soldiers. They were forced to postpone, but the bad weather screened them better than they had dared hope. If they could not move their "horse" with favorable tides, the invasion would have to be postponed for a month. The effort of keeping the secret, known to more than 100,000 men, would have been impossible, and morale would have fallen to abysmal depths. The channel tides rose nineteen feet twice a day. The men had to be landed at a precise time, thirty minutes after dawn. At low tides, the boats could not approach the beach, and soldiers, heavily loaded with arms and supplies, would have drowned. The Germans had positioned obstacles so a time had to be set between high and low tides when these obstacles could be seen and avoided.

The Adriatic waters that Odysseus sailed could hardly have been more hazardous. The engineers had thirty minutes to demolish those obstacles. Despite miserable weather, the decision was made. Eisenhower said, "June sixth." The armada headed out into the drizzly weather. If postponed, unmanned German rockets would have rained down on the craft, and by June sixteenth, a fierce storm hit the channel and demolished many supply ships. Goering, the German air commander, made a serious blunder—one of many. He could not believe ships would cross the channel under such conditions. He kept his Luftwaffe grounded. Rommel was spending a relaxing weekend at his old home, and the German troops sat bored in their bunkers on the Normandy coast.

VIII
On the Beach

Just after 3:30 A.M., the men were called to battle stations, the airborne divisions had dropped on the objective. Jack had not slept. He stood with his sleepy troops around him, too excited to sleep, too geared up for action. Almost two years of inaction had brought him to an almost uncomfortable pitch. He had no thought of anything but the upcoming battle. Von Rundstedt, the German general, at Saint-Germain near Paris, thought the paratroops were only a diversion, a diversion from an Allied landing at Pas de Calais. Of such are the results of human miscalculation. Thirteen hundred RAF planes blanketed the French coast, followed by a wave of American spitfires. The Omaha beach "horse" fell hopelessly behind schedule. Rommel and seasoned soldiers were defending, and Allied casualties were heavy.

Fortunately for Jack and his men, General Bradley had sent him and his troops to Utah beach, where the landings were opposed only by second-rate troops, who collapsed quickly. General Theodore Roosevelt Jr. was a brigadier with this group. He was a seasoned campaigner and heartened his troops with humor and bravery not always evident in some of the other top officers. General Ridgway's Eighty-second Airborne was scattered due to the inclement weather, but they were able to establish themselves at Sainte-Mère-Église, where Jack wearily stumbled into an abandoned wine cellar. He and a number of his exhausted men were finally able to doze off.

Goering neglected to throw air power against the landings, expecting Rommel to push the Allies back into the channel. He procrastinated long enough to let the troops establish a firm foothold in France. During this time, Jack became close to General Huebner. He had come up through the ranks and was known as "the soldiers' general." He was very concerned about all the men in his command and became a role model for Jack.

During the hectic first days on the beaches, General Huebner placed considerable responsibility on Jack and his reconnaissance outfit. The Germans had flooded the surrounding fields to force the Americans onto the narrow, mined roads, but the Omaha and Utah forces linked up by June tenth, and the fate of the empire of Hitler's dreams was sealed. The invasion was a success.

As the troops moved up the narrow roads from Caen to the Cotentin Peninsula, the German officers hesitated. They could not believe that the important port of Cherbourg could be sealed off by the advancing Allied troops. Another war may have been lost "for want of a nail . . ." but the Allied invasion succeeded because of a series of errors by the German high command. Hitler had intuitively believed that the invasion would come on the beaches of Normandy but bowed to the flawed suppositions of his generals. If he had prevailed, the outcome would have been far different. Perhaps the excesses perpetrated by Hitler and his psychotic dreams and perverted henchmen had subconsciously created in his better officers a hope that, although the assassination plot against Hitler had failed, the Allies would force their shattered homeland to its knees and end the debacle. No civilized man, and these officers were too intelligent not to realize this, could live under such a demented and subhuman regime.

The cavalryman's ability to sleep in the saddle was transferred to the armored vehicles. After a night on the front lines, Jack found that he could sleep almost anywhere. A bigger problem was the inability to bathe. On the trip across the channel, water was saved for the first wave of wounded. Once the beachhead was secured, there was no time or water for bathing purposes. It was three weeks before they had a shower. Jack's unit went ahead of the infantry to smoke out the enemy and often found itself trying to dislodge 88-mm guns that killed several troopers and wounded others. Jack's charmed life was still intact, but he suffered every wound with his men. He was devoutly thankful that horses were not involved in a battle they could not have survived.

He felt great respect for General Bradley when he said, "War is as much a conflict of passion as it is of force. No commander can become a strategist until he first knows his men. Far from being a handicap to command, compassion is the measure of it." Jack was such a commander to gladden Bradley's heart. Indeed, he was recognized as such when he met General Bradley many years later in the Pentagon. During the blistering battles, his troops would follow him anywhere as did Odysseus's woebegone followers.

The reconnaissance outfit cooked meals on small gasoline stoves from the canned C rations, vegetable and meat stew or baked beans and bacon. There were no chow lines or cooks here. The food was monotonous but welcome. This was hardly the biggest problem the men had to face. They were in almost constant action as a small armored force and some infantry emerged from the beachhead. They began to function as the reconnaissance unit they were trained to be.

One of their greatest problems was a cultural or ethnic one they had never seen before. French farmers had long made stiff hedgerows the boundary markers for their farms. These were a major obstacle and slowed the advance of Jack's unit. The raised and ditched rows of thorny, deep-rooted shrubs created more problems than the metal spikes sunk by the Germans at the beaches. The hedgerows frustrated the tanks and upended their bellies to the enemy guns like overturned turtles.

General Bradley was summoned by General Gerow to see something in Jack's battalion. A little, bowlegged sergeant, a former horse trooper, had fastened a tusklike device on a crossbar on the front of Jack's light tanks. It pushed right through the hedgerows, a simple device for moving an army that had been baffled for five weeks. For his inventiveness, the sergeant received the Legion of Merit, but in subsequent fighting, four months later, he lost a leg in the Huertgen Forest and was sent home. Within a week, most tanks were fitted with the device, and the army moved forward with Jack's unit in the lead.

There were many near misses for Jack as the battle lines seesawed back and forth, the Germans helping immeasurably by their inability to realize the objectives of the Allied armies. There were even bombings of the Allied troops by their own planes; the adversaries and their lines were so close together. One day when Jack was inspecting the lines, a soldier in a communication truck asked him to have coffee with them. He declined, saying he wanted to check the front lines but would stop on his way back. When he returned, there was no truck, no soldiers, only a deep bomb crater.

The troop was in the forefront of the fighting when Jack's luck ran out, his Achilles' heel was struck in a most unprepossessing way. He was standing by his command car some distance behind the lines, when a stray bullet ricocheted off the vehicle and tore through his right arm. Bone was smashed with nerves and vessels severed. He was hurried back to England after first-aid treatment and placed in the amputee ward. Army medics wanted to amputate the arm, but he refused vehemently. Fortunately for him, consistent with the luck that so often attended him, a West Point colonel, also a surgeon and a former quarterback on an army team, realized what the loss of an arm would mean to this man, who had played professional football. He knew that such drastic surgery would leave a mental as well as a physical handicap. He overruled the other surgeons and undertook this endeavor to treat the wound conservatively.

For four long months, this active man remained in the hospital near Oxford, chafing to get back to battle. His nemesis was a stereotypical, officious, regular army nurse whom he took great glee in baiting. Jokes were his life blood, and he played many on her, much to the delight of his fellow invalids. He and another soldier escaped from the ward, dressed only in their pajamas and bathrobes, and visited a local pub. Sneaking back up a deserted road, they met a general in a command car and stood at attention to salute. They must have been a ridiculous sight. Jack never told me what happened after that escapade, but he was not demoted, so his wound probably saved him from disciplinary action.

Before he was due to be discharged and sent back to the States, he and another officer stole uniforms in their rank from the medical officers' quarters, commandeered a jeep and sat off for the front lines. M.P.s stopped soldiers traveling away from the battle lines but paid no attention to those going toward the front. They rejoined their units without incident. The jeep somehow found its way back to its original post as did the purloined uniforms. No story was ever told about the aftermath of this flight from authority, and also, no mention was made on efficiency reports and no disciplinary action taken. General Huebner was undoubtedly glad to get one of his favorite commanders back, with no questions asked. However, due to the severity of his wound, he was assigned to a reassignment depot and thence to an M.P. battalion. He was upset as the armies moved ahead without him. While he had been hospitalized, much drama had taken place.

Media fables accompanied General Patton as he advanced toward Paris, but the First Army suffered almost twice the casualties sustained by that general's army, as the First cleared the way for his triumphant march into the "city of light." Actually a great problem was to evolve, as the starving Parisians needed everything. Their needs would mean the substitution of supplies for the gasoline needed to continue the final march toward subjugation of the German army. The logistics of such a quandary caused many headaches for the Allied commanders. However, many of these Americans were the sons of fathers who had captured the hearts of Parisians in a previous war. Perhaps some were the sons of French war brides, so Paris, although strategically unimportant, was a target of their emotions.

By August 21, Patton's army was north and south of the city. General Patton was stimulated by the black and screaming headlines, and he chafed under the censorship that was imposed to keep Hitler from exact knowledge of the size of the forces opposing him. Headlines made him appear reckless, and his superiors had great difficulty restraining him. German General Kluge ordered the garrison in Paris to split up into small groups to attempt an escape, and he committed suicide, a sacrifice to Hitler's grandiloquent scheme.

When General Bradley was asked which division could have the honor of taking Paris, he responded to the correspondents, "Why don't you take it yourselves? You've got enough correspondents here to do it! I might as well tell you, we're not at all anxious to take Paris right now."

He was afraid that due to bombed-out rail lines and bridges, the liberation of Paris's millions would cause the supply lines to dry up, as indeed they did. The Allied troops were halted by a gas drought just short of the German's Siegfried line. While the Allied troops remained outside the city, the resistance fighters began to fire on the German enemy.

The French patience had worn thin. In order to save Paris from the German orders to leave nothing behind but rubble on retreat, the German commander agreed to surrender to the Allied forces. A French force under General LeClerc was allowed to be the first into the city. His troops went through a wall of jubilant citizens who met his soldiers with wine and celebration. When the Americans threatened to be the first to enter and take the German commander prisoner, LeClerc's soldiers hurried to the Hotel Meurice. With smoke grenades, they drove the Germans out of their headquarters to the surrender meeting, where they turned the city over to the French.

Jack, as an M.P. commander, was present when the celebrations began in earnest. He felt the French apparently loved celebrations and quickly forgot the privations and loss of dignity during the occupation, but they also quickly forgot those who gave their lives to make the celebration possible.

The M.P.s were very busy, and Jack was forced into situations he did not enjoy. He often remarked, "Men don't change their nature when they put on a uniform." There was rape, robbery, absent without leave, and a great deal of black-market trading of American supplies of candy, food, and all the things the Germans had siphoned off from their captive countries. The events he hated most were the hangings, which occurred as sentences for capital crimes. He sat on the court-martials and had to be present at the carrying out of the sentences. As bloody as the Normandy landings had been and all the combat mayhem, he hated the death sentences most. Fortunately, they were few in number. He was responsible for a large sector of liberated France known as the Chanor sector of the European Theater of Operations. It was a major assignment, and his efficiency reports indicated an excellent performance. He was given a treasured French decoration.

As the armies moved on to the German border, he was moved to Antwerp as executive officer of that liberated port. This was particularly important because winter was making the captured beaches useless. It was necessary to maintain one of the best-equipped ports for the tons of supplies and gasoline needed for the final push to Germany. Jack fretted his absence from combat and the exhilaration of the final thrust. He missed the Ardennes fighting, where his odyssey might have come to an end, as the casualties were very heavy. As it turned out, he was spared to fight another day. For his efforts in Belgium, he was awarded the Legion of Honor of Leopold II, a spectacular decoration, which he hid with others in the lowest drawer of his retirement secretary.

Before it was all over in Europe and Hitler had committed suicide in his bunker, Jack had one more chance to fight. On December sixteenth, a week before Christmas, von Rundstedt tried a last ditch assault on the extended American and British lines. He created a bulge not too far from Liège, where Jack happened to be. All troops of every type, cooks, clerks, and military police, were called in to man the cold, wet lines. It became the infamous Battle of the Bulge, the last gasp of der Führer's dream of empire. It was as though the Allied troops had had enough of this terrible war and decided to mop up that German attack and get it over with. It would, however, take seven weeks more before the winter offensive could continue its march to the Ruhr and Rhine Rivers. Jack had participated in one more battle but then returned to his Belgian post.

Scylla and Charybdis reared up to try to trap him. Alcoholism was a continuing problem in the military, and Jack was not completely immune, although he never allowed liquor to interfere with his duties. One of his polo buddies, however, was a severe alcoholic, and Jack had to rescue him from army discipline many times. Cognac was cheap and available, and Jack imbibed his share until a rash was identified as caused by the liquor. This stopped him as he was very conscious of his health. His crony's drinking became unmanageable, and he was shipped back to America.

Jack's M.P. command created a great many pressures. One of these was the arrangement of President Truman's visit to Potsdam. Security was tight and totally his responsibility. After liberation, stiff currency reforms were instituted in Belgium to weed out inflated paper money and the consequent profiteers who are always present after a debacle. Some of Jack's duties included rounding up these ghouls who were enjoying the muddled European situation. Lighter assignments included keeping occupation forces of officers and men from the delights of Brussels' brothels, which were flourishing. Later, whenever he smelled the perfume, Charlie, he said it reminded him of those dubious establishments from which he evacuated even high-ranking officers just prior to a military police raid. His own fastidious inclinations saved him from infection even as Odysseus deflected the perfidious delights of the Sirens.

Campagnes pour la libération de la France
(1944 - 1945)

Décret N° 2

*Le Général de Gaulle,
Président du Gouvernement Provisoire de la République Française.*

Décrète :

Est décoré de la Médaille de la Reconnaissance Française,

Lieut-Colonel John L. LEE, O-275094, CHANOR

" Pour services exceptionnels de Guerre rendus au
" cours des opérations de libération de la France."

PARIS, le 29 Septembre 1945

P.A.Le General d'Armee JUIN

Le Ministre de la Défense Nationale

a l'honneur de faire savoir _____ au _____

Lieutenant-Colonel, John, L., L E E ,

que, par Arrêté de S.A.R., le Prince Régent, du 1.6.1946, n° 2392,

il a été nommé

OFFICIER DE L'ORDRE DE LEOPOLD II

en reconnaissance des services rendus à la Belgique.

      Il s'estime heureux de pouvoir lui adresser ses félicitations au sujet de cette nomination.

IX
VE Day and Beyond

On May 7, 1945, General Jodl and Admiral Von Friedburg signed an unconditional surrender at Eisenhower's headquarters. They tried to stall so as to move German soldiers, equipment, and supplies, as well as civilians, away from the Russian front and occupation. Apparently they did not trust the Russians and preferred the Allies' tender mercies. Subsequent mass graves found in 1990, after the collapse of the Soviet Union, proved their concern well-founded, but Eisenhower refused any delay.

The European adventure was over, with 135,576 Americans dead and 440,000 wounded, a terrible price to pay to defeat a single madman with dreams of conquest.

While some of the commanding officers were transferred to the Pacific theater, Jack remained in Brussels. There were many problems remaining, even though the atomic bomb ended the Japanese kamikaze efforts on August 9 and V-J Day occurred on August 19.

The cessation of hostilities on both fronts meant little to Penny personally, although she shared the general relief that the home front jubilantly celebrated. She had had no news of Jack for several years. Although there was an empty spot in her emotions every day and every night whenever she had time to think, she was neither an optimist nor a pessimist. She faced an uncertain world and future realistically. She knew that the more one tried to make expectations match reality, the more unhappy one's life might be. A suitor was waiting. She was honest, telling him that she had been deeply in love and was not sure she would ever be able to recapture those feelings. He persisted, however. He was a displaced veteran, a naval officer, and an attorney in civilian life. He apparently felt she was a strong shoulder to lean on as he attempted to put his life back together.

He was in New York, terminating naval contracts for which he had the legal background. They had met when Penny was particularly vulnerable. He had the advantage of returning to his home three thousand miles away from Jack's home area, where Jack might eventually return. This man also had the advantage of a career to which he would presumably return. She followed him, on his discharge, to the West Coast, where, some six months later, on January 7, 1947, she stopped knitting and unraveling and was married.

She did not know that Jack was on leave, the first one he had taken in four, long, war-scarred years. He was to be reassigned and arrived in the United States on December 6, one month before Penny's marriage. He was told, by well-meaning friends, when he inquired, that she had married and was living on the West Coast. That misinformation, while unintentional, caused long years of unhappiness for both.

After his accumulated leave was over, Jack saw little reason to return to his civilian occupation of engineer. The camaraderie, discipline, and excitement of the military appealed to him more than did nine-to-five employment. He had no wife and family to support, so he applied for a regular army appointment in October 1947. His long and well-documented exemplary service was equated to attendance at command school. His efficiency reports were outstanding and constantly mentioned his tact and his ability to command respect from enlisted men and officers alike. With unaccustomed foresight, the high command gave him regular status, which was unusual, since demobilization was much more common as wartime needs diminished.

His first assignment was as liaison officer to National Guard units in the middle-Atlantic states. A supreme irony was that the inept colonel of pre-Pearl Harbor days signed a commendation and specifically mentioned Jack's superior performance during a regular army training encampment at a National Guard facility. The old recriminations did not survive the war, and the colonel, now a general, had no particular axe to grind.

Penny knew nothing of these changes or of his whereabouts. She was embroiled in a mockery of a marriage with a bigoted and incipiently psychotic husband. He did not take up his prewar career; he refused many law cases that former clients asked him to pursue, saying that he was only interested in corporate and real estate law and considered divorce cases and criminal law practice beneath him. His former partners, none of whom saw service, also did little to help him reestablish himself. He blamed much of his inability to practice as he wished on Penny, saying that he would be ashamed to take her to the prestigious downtown club he had formerly frequented.

Penny sentimentally decided that his aged mother was unable to care for herself and brought her into their home. This drain on her time, as well as a full-time position in the local visiting nurse service, left her little time for grief or self-pity. There were many men still in uniform, and every time she saw the familiar khaki emblazoned with battle ribbons, she looked long and hard. Mercifully, she never knew that Jack had returned a month before her ill-considered marriage. If he had given any sign of remembrance of their lost love, she would have fled from her mistake to join him, but it did not happen.

In addition to her already heavy load, a long-time patient who needed frequent visits from Penny to alleviate pain made a will naming Penny as guardian of her children. She felt that Penny, as a nurse, and her husband, as an attorney, would be able to either care for them or see that they were properly placed. One does not walk away from an animal shelter without a pleading dog. Penny could not refuse this plaintive request although it took her by surprise and her home life was very difficult as it was. Willing a child is not legal, but the mother's relatives were only too happy to have someone else worry about two young children. Since it was obvious that she would never have Jack's children and had no desire to make the mistake of trying to cement a bad marriage by having children in her present circumstances, Penny welcomed these waifs. Their father was aged and blind and had died six months before his wife. Penny arranged for their care at a children's home, since the boy was not of school age and she was working full time. The social worker there was dubious about their soon-to-be foster father's mental stability. Penny was too close to the situation to realize how unstable he really was. It was a decision she was not to regret although finances and their constant care was most difficult. They were always there needing her when her life looked most bleak.

Her husband took little notice of his mother or the children, although he liked the little girl. He disliked the boy, who had mild cerebral palsy, because it was obvious that he could never be a famous athlete and "make a father proud." He returned home in the afternoons and increasingly isolated himself from the family needs and finances with cigars, a glass of wine, and his dreams.

The family existed on Penny's small salary as the debts piled up.

X
Circe Spins a Web

Undaunted by the wide Atlantic, the "French divorcée," described by the wounded returning soldiers from Jack's original troop, decided upon a carefully planned assault on the genial colonel and America. He must have had some misgivings about her status and past, since he dispatched a young lieutenant to London to look into her background. That gentleman must have made a very superficial job of investigation, since developments much later revealed a very checkered past and many lies.

Jack's mother, however, bemused by the title this woman claimed, Lady Something-or-Other, continuously praised her to the skies, feeling such a fine lady would add to her own social standing. After all, she herself had married a "Kentucky colonel," who proceeded to waste Jack's allotment and any funds remaining from those left her by Jack's father. After she made two transatlantic trips, Jack finally succumbed, and they were married in 1949.

A lawyer and investigator notified him that his first wife had gone through with a divorce and had remarried. Then his troubles really began.

He was assigned to the New York-New Jersey National Guard as Regular Army adviser and was stationed in New York City. His superiors, mindful of his excellent ratings, stipulated that he was to remain on the overseas duty list for reassignment in 1951. During this period, Penny's sister-in-law actually played in a bridge group with Circe but did not connect the names.

While on Stateside duty, Jack realized he had made a serious mistake in his marriage. His wife remained a British citizen. She would never allow him to accompany her when she registered as an alien, which was required at that time. With his customary lack of insight where women were concerned, probably a male failing, he never questioned her secrecy until it was too late to change matters.

He discovered many years later, after her death, that she had lied about her age by thirteen years, being much older than he and, more important, had not been divorced from the Indian army colonel who had given her his title. Another marriage in England had been annulled when that spouse discovered the bigamous truth. Her London lawyers notified her, under her maiden name, that the colonel had died but only after she had been married to Jack for some time.

Jack found all this out twenty-five years later when going through her effects to dispose of them. A small, locked suitcase contained all the incriminating evidence. His marriage could have destroyed the army career he loved. He was impotently furious. One would have expected her to have destroyed the evidence of this bigamous situation and her passport as well, which indicated her rather questionable past in the Far East, in places like Macao. That she retained so much of this material was probably part of a beginning psychosis, which eventually became full-blown and completed the destruction of a miserable marriage.

Jack's attention to duty requirements and subsequent assignments after his marriage allowed him to absent himself from his dilemma. He was detached to the famous Eighty-second Airborne Division at Fort Bragg to help with the division's cooperation with armored units with which he was so closely identified during the landing and combat. He was next posted to Camp Polk, Louisiana, where he learned to jump. He was forced into social situations with his wife, which had always bored him and which he now hated. He was suspicious of her actions and suspected infidelity but, characteristically, put off any unpleasantness, using duty and official absences to avoid confrontation. To absent himself even more, he took a weekend job of crop dusting. He loved flying over the treetops and the excitement of possible danger. The warhorse was bored with the routine and inactivity of peacetime.

He was given command of a battalion of black troops. At this time, the army was under de facto segregation. President Truman tried to talk about desegregation, but it was ten years before the civil rights movement allowed the army to establish integrated facilities and troop makeup. He enjoyed commanding these troops, but there was harassment from several white units. They played unpleasant tricks, like digging up lawns and flowers that had been laboriously planted around the black barracks and other not-so-hidden, Klan-like activities. With tact and clever response, he was able to defuse otherwise tense situations and received many commendations.

XI
A New War

During World War II, when Russia entered the war against Japan, Japanese Korea was arbitrarily divided at the 34th parallel. The Russians occupied the industrial North and the Western Allies the rural South. The seeds of conflict were sown. The United States wanted a unified peninsula with a democratic government, fairly elected. Stalin had other ideas. The United States had occupation forces in South Korea but wanted to withdraw them as soon as possible. The Defense Department felt that it was a militarily indefensible area. They had only 20,000 troops in the occupation of Japan. MacArthur had an attenuated force, the Eighth Army, in Japan and was trying to train on a crowded island of defeated people. His troops were green and flabby, some even had Japanese servants. It must have been obvious to Russian military advisors that adventurism would pay off on this ill-favored finger of land.

In North Korea, Stalin was laying plans for yet another puppet government, as he had in Eastern Europe. It was backed by a growing Moscow bureaucracy and military buildup. By now, the Soviet Union, once a Western ally, was a main enemy. Stalin's plan to take over the whole Korean peninsula and set up a puppet with access to the sea was obvious. With their constant preoccupation with containing communism and its ideology, the United States government decided to help implement what was euphemistically called a police action by the United Nations. It was a very difficult problem, both logistically and militarily. The country was extremely rugged and, in many cases, very hostile. Communist Chinese and Koreans looked very much alike to U.S. G.I.s, and infiltration was ever-present. The climate was very hot in summer and freezing cold in winter. Odysseus's problems fighting before the walls of Troy must have presented like quandaries. Was it all worth it? While Jack was enjoying the "blue northers," bitterly cold winds sweeping across the prairies from Canada into Louisiana and Texas, the conflict in Korea was spreading. General Bradley, at this time, chief of staff, was quoted as saying "that with federal budget-cutting, the peace-time army couldn't fight its way out of a paper bag."

The Eighty-second Airborne was the only combat-ready unit. General Woodruff, the commanding general of this unit, and Jack had become good friends. Their greatest entertainment was to parachute jump together. The general insisted that on his birthday he would jump for each year of his age, and he was close to retirement! Jack was his enthusiastic companion. This was another way to avoid his increasingly unpleasant home life. He was aware that she was finding other recreation than bridge. Confrontation over their situation in a politicized army would not only have solved nothing, but would have been less favorably viewed by his superiors than a wandering wife. Wives had always been a problem in army posts and were usually regarded as excess baggage to be tolerated.

The peacetime army was faltering under bureaucratic fumbling in Washington. Most of the defense of the United States and Europe was focused on the Soviet capabilities. The Russians exploded an atomic bomb in 1949. Spies within British Intelligence were responsible for leaking information and providing the Soviets with the technique and plans for an even more destructive bomb, the H-bomb. The little "haberdasher" in Washington, President Truman, made courageous decisions to try to keep the U.S. militarily strong enough to counteract Soviet expansionism. As usual, there was considerable dissension and competition between the services for defense dollars.

None of this internecine squabbling was lost on the rank-and-file soldiers and their immediate superior officers. Many of the latter found it hard to maintain discipline. Jack was distressed at the positions juggled about in Washington, especially where they applied to some of his friends and the generals he respected. In spite of the situation, however, he was able to retain his personal commitment to the army. This filtered down to his junior officers and, through them, to the enlisted men.

Penny, far away on the West Coast, knew nothing of the Pentagon's problems and had little time to read newspapers or listen to news broadcasts. Her married life had really ceased to exist. Her husband, severely displaced from his former legal career, floundered in civilian life. He had had several lucrative offers to use his legal background but had constantly insisted he wanted to practice as he wished and would not work for anyone or any corporation.

Penny worked hard at her public health job and struggled to stretch her meager salary to cover household expenses, with no help from her spouse. The children and her bedridden mother-in-law kept her so busy, she had little time to think, and her pride kept her from admitting what a terrible mistake she had made. She knitted occasionally and unraveled when the garment was unsatisfactory. She had no idea of the parallel with another Penelope.

At the same time that arguments continued in Washington, a further problem was developing in the Far East. During the United States preoccupation with the growing Soviet threats in Eastern Europe, China, under the Nationalists, was being overrun by a new and menacing Communist figure, Mao Tse-tung. Mao captured Mukden in Manchuria and set the stage for the next chapter in Jack's odyssey. General MacArthur, sometimes described by his fellow officers as a megalomaniac, wanted an early peace treaty signed with Japan. He refused to consider giving up any of his small force to Stateside requests for a cut in the military establishment.

He felt communism in the Far East was as great a threat if not greater than that in Europe. Subsequent events bore out his contention. The United States thought a perimeter of bases in the Philippines, on Okinawa, Formosa, and Japan were vital and proceeded to help the Nationalists protect the airfields on Formosa. These had originally been built by the Japanese invasion forces.

In June 1950, the Communist North Korean army invaded South Korea, and a new conflict began. While all this was going on in Korea, Communists from China were infiltrating Vietnam. This action also threatened Indochina. At the same time, it was difficult to know what the next Russian move might be. For the time being, it was decided in Washington to restrict U.S. intervention in Korea to air and naval power in the area. However, the subsequent rout of the (R.O.K.) Republic of Korea forces made the U.S. Joint Chiefs of Staff reluctantly agree to commit ground forces to keep North Korea above the 38th parallel, the dividing line. This proved a much harder task than anyone envisioned in 1950. The commanders were warned to keep U.S. troops away from any confrontation on the Russian and Manchurian borders.

To an Irish army warhorse like Jack, snorting and stamping at Camp Polk, this was a new challenge. He had no desire to remain Stateside in his unpleasant marriage. Life would again feel like living with a new fight brewing. Fortunately, a frustrated and overworked Penny, on the West Coast, did not even visualize this new involvement as one that would include the man she had never expected to see again.

In his diary, Truman blew off steam about MacArthur, labeling him privately, "a play-actor and a bunco man." He went on to scribble, "I don't see how a country can produce such men as Robert E. Lee, John J. Pershing, Eisenhower, and Bradley, and at the same time produce Custers, Pattons, and MacArthurs!"

The biggest worry in Washington at this time was that the United States might be dragged through the Korean borders into a war with Communist China. This situation, the Joint Chiefs of Staff and the president knew, would give great joy to the Soviets. MacArthur did not seem to agree with this view of the U.S. predicament. The Washington establishment also did not realize that this was not a standard war. It was labeled a United Nations police action, but it was spearheaded by a traditional soldier, MacArthur, who felt his role of theater commander gave him exceptional latitude. General Bradley was to concede later, in his autobiography, that the Joint Chiefs indulged in "wishful thinking" and committed a grave error. Intelligence was woefully inadequate and did not know of the size of the forces Chinese Communists had thrown into North Korea. Those forces ultimately forced the U.N. troops, mostly U.S., back to the 38th parallel, which they felt could be defended. An incompetent general was killed in a jeep accident, reminiscent of Patton's death. This allowed General Matt Ridgway to be placed in command of the Eighth Army. His new assignment had a profound effect on Jack's future.

MacArthur had lost all his previous optimism and wanted to risk an all-out war with China. The Soviet Union was lurking in the shadows and was not at all afraid to launch W.W. III. Ridgway's Eighth Army had retaken Seoul and had, to all intents, bailed out MacArthur, the Supreme Commander. That gentleman seemed resigned to leave it all to "Matt." He possibly had his eye on the 1952 presidential election. He had been fooled by the Chinese generals, and his pride was warping his judgment; generals are just as prone to errors of omission and commission as the rest of us. Unfortunately, many men died because of those "errors." It is remarkable that the United States had survived some of its conflicts. The only explanation may be that the enemy commanders, also human, made mistakes of their own.

It was the first time in history that concerted international action was considered. It was important to fight a limited war, in contrast to all-out war. Thermonuclear weapons were now a reality and a threat to the entire planet. It was clear that military strength alone would not ensure victory, if, indeed, such was ever possible.

While perceptive people, in and out of government, realized there was a new world alignment, it is doubtful that old-line soldiers, such as Jack, spent much time in philosophizing about the political aspects of this far-off conflict. They were too busy with training troops to utilize ever-new mechanical instruments of destruction. As in World War II, the war seemed far away. The Trojan horse of an ancient war would not work here. General Ridgway was ordered to the NATO command as General Eisenhower left to campaign for the presidency. This was a new age when Fortress America had to join world-sanctioned "police actions."

Few people in America, Penny as well, did not consider this Far Eastern conflict their problem. They were recovering from the last war and were very isolationist in their views. Penny's husband refused to consider returning to the practice of law unless he was financially able to reject cases he did not want. He took on commercial projects for which he was legally qualified but lacked financial backing. Bankers tried to tell him this was the case, but he continued to reach for financial stars. The bankers even asked Penny to come in so they could warn her of impending disaster. She now had four "children" to care for. The only positive aspect of the situation was that she was too busy to mourn the past. She did not even have time to knit anymore.

In fact, by this time, the debts had become so troublesome that Penny contemplated pawning a sapphire ring from a relative. Instead, she found that a small local hospital was short of help. She applied for part-time weekend work and was able to spell the overworked nurses in the newborn nursery. They were grateful for the free weekend and she was grateful for the money. It was night duty, so every week she missed a night's sleep even as the household responsibilities continued in the daytime. It was rugged, but she loved handling the unsullied newborns before inept parents or society molded them into conformity or worse.

General Van Fleet replaced General Ridgway in the chain of command. He asked for Jack and reinstituted his overseas assignment. In forty-eight hours, Jack packed, flew from Camp Polk, and arrived in Korea. Seven hundred sixty-eight thousand Eighth Army and R.O.K. troops faced nearly a million Chinese and North Korean troops. The populous Chinese constantly replaced those lost who were callously placed in the line of U.N. fire. There were heaps of dead Chinese each time they withdrew.

Jack was given the task of reorganizing the Eighth Army and correlating relations between the U.N. and U.S. fighting men. The cultural differences between Ethiopian soldiers, for example, and those of European and U.S. troops were enormous. Food preferences necessitated finding unusual rations. Goats, sheep, and other sources of meat had to be obtained by procurement officers. This was difficult in an Asiatic country. The Dutch wanted milk, the French wanted wine, the Moslems no pork, and the Hindus no beef. The Orientals wanted more rice, and the Europeans more bread. Uniforms were important to each country's contribution to the forces. This was something that had not been contemplated when assembling a multinational army. Shoes had to be extra wide for the Turks and narrow and short for the Filipinos and Thais. American clothing was far too big for the Eastern men. Scandinavian and Canadian contingents could adapt easily. The logistical problems, amazingly enough, were finally sorted out by the officers under Jack's command. He who had rarely considered foods, cooking, or even entered a grocery store, learned along with his fellow officers.

Truce negotiations had been seesawing back and forth. The Chinese and North Korean negotiators used all kinds of propaganda techniques to stall any forward movement. They found the 150,000 Communist prisoners of war held on off-shore islands by the U.N. forces a convenient way of fomenting problems. Of course, they did not advertise that they took few U.N. prisoners, preferring to keep their slender rice rations for themselves. Either they preferred to overlook Geneva conventions or did not even know such humanitarian protocols existed.

It was a peculiar war, full of unexpected hazards, of which

logistics was only one. Everywhere Jack went on inspection, strange things happened. Wine bottles on tables were booby-trapped, even in the officers' mess, probably by infiltrating Chinese. On one occasion, he was inspecting facilities in Inchon. Three sides of the headquarters were protected by fortifications and guards. The fourth side on the water was unguarded. He questioned the safety of the installation. He was assured that the Chinese would never attack by sea, and he was invited to spend the night, but went on to other posts. During that same night, the Chinese did attack by sea, and all personnel were killed.

There were other environmental and cultural concerns that were conducive to serious effects on the U.S. and U.N. soldiers. Vegetables grew to enormous size in the Korean soil but could not be procured for the foreign troops' mess. They were fertilized by what was euphemistically called "night-soil," human excreta containing all sorts of parasites and bacteria to which the foreign troops were not immune. In the officers' mess, a Korean bartender was drafted for the R.O.K. army. He was back in a month, sans civilian clothes, ready to go back to work. Unfortunately, the army could not keep him. He was suffering from terminal tuberculosis.

Another bartender realized a new source of income. He took empty club-soda bottles with American labels, filled them with water from the grossly contaminated Han River, used capsules to counterfeit effervescence, and served it to the officers in mixed drinks. Perhaps the alcohol disguised the taste and lessened the lethal quality of the drinks. However, some of the officers came down with unusual maladies that the U.N. medical officers could find no way to treat, and some died of these rare diseases.

Housing in this extremely hot or bitterly cold climate also posed many problems. Heat pipes were buried under cement floors where maintenance was impossible. A fellow officer refused to take Room 13 in their barracks. Jack offered his less ominous room. In the morning, the superstitious officer was found dead from fumes from a defective heater. Then there was kimchi, a fermented concoction of cabbage among other things. The Korean cleaning women stashed this very odorous national dish in the officers' closets, since their heated rooms generated more fermentation than was available in the unheated or destroyed civilian homes. The smell was indescribable, and since communication was difficult, the kimchi remained, but the officers never again wanted to eat cabbage. In spite of all rules, fraternizing with Korean women was occurring, and the forbidden vegetables were often consumed. A very serious and usually fatal blood disease began to appear.

On rest and recreation leave in Tokyo, Jack felt too isolated from the conflict. With his customary reluctance for casual sex and his fear of venereal disease, he had little interest in sake or ministrations of the ubiquitous geisha girls. There was little else to do in the city or, at least, little to take the place of his comrades and the need for constant action. He was anxious to get back to his duties, so he cut short his unwanted vacation and hitched a ride on a small plane while some of his fellow officers waited for a transport. The transport was destroyed in midair with all passengers killed. He assumed, as did most soldiers, that when a weapon had their name on it, there was no escape. Until that time they were relatively safe.

During the severe Korean winter of 1952 to 1953, the defense lines were in constant movement and assault. Jack found himself on frozen hillsides in temperatures sometimes at minus forty-five degrees. They could light no fires that would alert Chinese patrols to their location. It became obvious that there was no way to force the locustlike hordes of Chinese from the peninsula, and constant action was needed to keep them above the truce line at Panmunjom. The Chinese commanders paid little heed to truces. The fighting foreshadowed the guerilla battles of the 1960s and beyond.

In April 1953, the Chinese and North Koreans decided to cry "victory" in what was a stalemate. Perhaps their home front was not happy with the heavy casualties. They began a series of attacks that would be their final offensive. In one of the last actions of the war, Jack found himself in the punchbowl, the forward line of troops defending a bridge that the Chinese decided to regain. On a mountain trail, he and his jeep driver raced ahead of the surging Chinese lines just before U.N. forces bombed that narrow road to halt the Chinese advance. On his way back and across a raging river, from the high mountain walls bordering the trail, a huge tiger, also fleeting the advancing hordes, sailed over their open jeep.

This last-ditch offensive by the Chinese gained several hills and ground along an eight-mile front, but the Communists lost about 7,300 dead, wounded, and missing. As usual, they did not feel the expenditure of so many, for such small gains were of little significance. Their burgeoning population increased the availability of *canonen* fodder and an Asiatic concept of *lebensraum*. Malthusian law was still in force. As population became unmanageable, war, disease, and famine resulted; the modern human family still apparently did not remember this medieval concept.

On July 19, a final cease-fire was agreed upon. It had been an international action for three years, one month, and two days. Jack was to spend two of those years in what he later described as the worst country on earth, hot in summer and frigid in winter, with miserable terrain and squalid cities. Surely Odysseus never felt those extremes in the Adriatic or the *Odyssey* never would have been written. Modern warfare allowed for much more savage and destructive engagements.

Jack's tour of duty, however, was not over with the guns' silence. He had several more contacts with Far Eastern philosophy and lurking problems. Syngman Rhee was president of South Korea. He gave lip service to the U.N. forces while stashing away a personal fortune of U.S. largesse in Switzerland. His Austrian wife was apparently equally duplicitous and untrustworthy. Jack had many occasions to see some strange behavior in the presidential palace. He was appointed liaison officer but was much disturbed by his inability to understand the Oriental mind and language, although most educated Koreans could at least understand English and many had studied in the United States. The First Lady of Korea was even more inscrutable, despite her European background. She behaved in ways even more Oriental than did her husband.

While this was going on, a mission was formed to visit the beleaguered French at Dien Bien Phu in Vietnam. Their task was to assess the situation with regard to the possibility of American help for the French forces. General Maxwell Taylor headed the mission. Jack was asked to accompany them. They left Korea and headed for another Asiatic involvement with the West. This time, it was the last gasp of a colonial power; the French, who had many entrenched interests in this colony, naturally did not want to relinquish them. The American group quickly determined they would not be able to maintain their position and reported this to Washington. They felt a civil war was brewing, and it would become a guerilla action. They felt America should not become involved, since they viewed it as an unwinnable situation. As so often happens, politics superseded judgment of those on the spot.

XII
The Long Way Back

The Legion of Merit citation read: "... distinguished himself by exceptionally meritorious performance ... and superior professional competence. ... [He] assumed responsibility for the reorganization of the troop basis for Eighth Army and R.O.K. Army to meet the demands of the critical tactical situation. ... His exemplary achievements contributed significantly to the U.N. campaign for world peace and reflect great credit upon himself and the military service."

Odysseus himself would have been proud of such words. Unfortunately, neither the siege of Troy nor the Korean conflict served to promote that mirage of a peaceful world. As to Jack's reaction to them, he placed the medal and citation in the bottom drawer of his secretary, not to be found until after his death.

An additional reward from the Korean conflict was an attack of malaria. Jack was given the option to fly back to the United States and enter a hospital for treatment or to take a troop transport and be treated en route. With a flashback to his World War II wound and his hospital experience at that time, he decided to take the only ship for a leisurely trip across the finally peaceful Pacific.

He embarked from Pusan, but the trip proved anything but peaceful. They were pounded by a typhoon in mid-Pacific, turned around to rescue a freighter in trouble, and eventually reached San Francisco. It was the end of a long combat mission in a hostile environment, and those who returned never forgot their experience and the men who were left behind, many thousands of them to whom nobody bothered to raise a monument.

Penny, of course, knew nothing of these events, since they were reported only sporadically as a distant and unwanted "police action." If she had time to think, she would have realized that Jack would have been involved, but she was detached from the image of the man she had loved so completely that, in self-defense, she rarely ever thought of those days of love and appreciation. She was getting a good deal of voiced gratitude from those she helped on the job and from the doctors with whom she worked, but little satisfaction at home, where an increasingly unstable man was mired deep in neurosis that eventually slipped over into paranoia. The children took much care in such a household, and her mother-in-law was senile and demanding. There was little she could do about the situation except work and provide a modicum of a home for all of them.

The aged woman was increasingly infirm and refused care from any one except Penny. She eventually became a twenty-four-hour charge for Penny, who was forced to place the old lady in a local nursing home. This proved to be the last straw to her husband's mental balance. He blamed her for the nursing home placement and sundry other charges, none with any foundation. Penny, who hated debts, was deluged by them, and her salary, slender as it was, was garnished to pay creditors. Fortunately, her employers valued her sufficiently to go to court in her behalf.

Obviously, the situation was at a point where a decision had to be made quickly, or, as Penny told the children, "Your father is sick, and if we stay here, we'll all be sick."

Her husband, apparently in the midst of his delusions, realized belatedly that he was in need of help. He sought out a minister who was also a trained family counselor. He told him he could not be married to Penny.

"She is not a Christian," he said.

The minister called Penny in for a conference. She came in

HEADQUARTERS
UNITED STATES ARMY FORCES, FAR EAST

CITATION FOR THE LEGION OF MERIT

Colonel JOHN L. LEE, 051088, General Staff, United States Army, distinguished himself by exceptionally meritorious conduct in the performance of outstanding service as Chief, Troop Control Division, G3 Section, Eighth Army, in Korea, from 14 October 1952 to 21 January 1954. Displaying astute judgment and superior professional competence, Colonel LEE assumed responsibility for the expedient reorganization of the troop basis for Eighth Army and the Republic of Korea Army to meet the urgent demands of the critical tactical situation. Through thorough study of the existing workload and personnel requirements and constant revision of operational procedures, he prepared sound policies relating to authorized strength ceilings of units and personnel changes within the commands. His comprehensive knowledge of organizational structure, keen analysis and judicious recommendations for manpower distribution effected optimum employment of the combat potential of the commands and insured the Army Commander the best possible balanced fighting force. Maintaining close coordination with higher headquarters and effecting prompt solution of complex problems incident to the reorganization and expansion of Eighth Army and the Republic of Korea Army, he assisted materially in the implementation of sound decisions which enhanced unification of effort and combat effectiveness of the combined commands and elicited high commendation from all with whom he served. Colonel LEE's skill, interest and enthusiasm, his thoroughness and attention to detail promoted increased efficiency of operations and the improved utilization of military manpower. His exemplary achievements contributed significantly to the United Nations' campaign for world peace and reflect great credit upon himself and the military service.

THE UNITED STATES OF AMERICA

TO ALL WHO SHALL SEE THESE PRESENTS, GREETING:
THIS IS TO CERTIFY THAT
THE PRESIDENT OF THE UNITED STATES OF AMERICA
AUTHORIZED BY ACT OF CONGRESS JULY 20, 1942
HAS AWARDED

THE LEGION OF MERIT

TO

Colonel John L. Lee, 051088, General Staff

FOR
EXCEPTIONALLY MERITORIOUS CONDUCT
IN THE PERFORMANCE OF OUTSTANDING SERVICES

Korea, 14 October 1952 - 21 January 1954

GIVEN UNDER MY HAND IN THE CITY OF WASHINGTON
THIS 22 d DAY OF January 19 54

Adjutant General
United States Army Forces, Far East

SECRETARY OF THE ARMY

uniform, unhappy to be called away from her work. After talking with her, the big bear of a man came around his desk, enfolded her in a great bear hug, and told her, "If you're not a Christian, I've never seen one!"

Jack was checked out at the Presidio. The malaria seemed to be in remission, and he was judged ready for reassignment. He was in no hurry to return to his unfaithful wife but could see little possibility of change in the domestic situation. It was ironic that, when he was in San Francisco, he was only a few hundred miles from Penny. Neither knew at that time what was going on in each other's lives, and there was no faithful son like Odysseus's to communicate with them both.

Eventually the reassignment orders came through. He was to report to Fort Knox to the weapons school, where he would be commandant. His students would be first and second lieutenants and noncommissioned officers. Who better to teach them the instruments of war? He enjoyed the experience, the students, and the proximity to Cincinnati, where he could see baseball games, the first in years. As an old semiprofessional ball player, it was good to be able to enjoy a past as well as a civilian pleasure. He had very frequent nightmares about the Korean War and, some, back to the Normandy landings but could expect little support from his spouse, whose only interest was in bridge games and officers' parties.

He realized she was having affairs but avoided any discussion, preferring to isolate himself in work and army routines. She once threatened to leave him and fly home to England. He should have encouraged this solution but was afraid he would be unable to trace her to obtain a divorce or ever know the status of his marriage. His fears were well founded as he later found out from her papers. He must have had an intuitive inkling of her previous history, but, again, procrastinated by living his own life and avoiding upsetting army brass and his own spotless record.

Generals and officials of the Pentagon as well as foreign army officers frequently came to Fort Knox as exchange personnel for instruction and observation of new equipment. He demonstrated for all these visitors and again received high commendations and ratings. One of the generals with whom he had served in both conflicts, General Ridgway, came to Fort Knox. He advised Jack to seek retirement. He told him that while he, the general, had recommended him for promotion to brigadier general, Jack would never receive that important appointment. The general and Eisenhower were not on friendly terms, and General Ridgway's whole promotion list would be consigned to the Oval Office waste basket.

Somehow the news of this would-be promotion leaked out, and Jack's hometown newspaper printed a picture and a premature article as though the promotion was a fact. It must have been a bitter postscript to his long years of service, but he never talked about it and just filed it away in that bottom drawer with all the medals and commendations. The star of course never materialized, but he disregarded the general's advice to retire from what had been his whole life. He went on with his assignment at Fort Knox until the next assignment came through.

XIII
The Long Way Home

With the transfer to Fort Knox, Jack began the long trek that would eventually lead him back to his home and the end of his wanderings. In 1923, as a young private, he had enlisted in the National Guard at Fort Riley, Kansas, to train with a cavalry unit. After 300-mile rides, maneuvers, and drills, he realized that the army and, specifically, the cavalry with its beautiful animals was where he wanted to be. His teachers became famous generals in World War II and Korea. Long after he left the prairies, he remembered the men he admired and the strategies they taught him. No one could have foreseen then that the bays, dappled duns, and the chestnut mounts would be replaced by iron horses and eventually the Trojan horse.

At Fort Knox, as well as in Europe and Korea, Jack fearlessly became what today would be called a whistle-blower. He wrote intelligent and well-constructed papers on several touchy subjects. He felt the occupation soldiers in Europe should be rotated home frequently and that families should not be moved at government expense with all the attendant facilities maintained in distant countries. With America's increasing police role, such ideas were apparently rethought long after he retired, after Korea, Vietnam, and the Middle East. The excessive costs of commissaries, schools, and clinics were eliminated. At Fort Knox, he wrote a well-researched paper on the decline of basic training and officer integrity in recording the results of such training.

He must have bloodied a few heads, but his innate tact,

diplomacy, and Irish humor accorded his ideas much more acceptance than the somewhat inept and bulldozer performance of today's critics of Pentagon and defense contract extravagance. Several examples of his observations, based on many years of experience, served to highlight his literary and diplomatic ability:

> We have been so intrigued by the atom bomb, atomic artillery and other new weapons that we appear to have forgotten that the rifleman and tank man still have the all important role of closing with the enemy, taking ground and holding it.

Another excerpt indicates that, while written in 1955, this expert soldier was far ahead of his time:

> Because of our great superiority in the air and our preponderance of fire power on the ground, our troops were rarely subjected to severe tests in World War II. Foreign observers, although high in their praise of our organization, coordination, fire power and logistics, were not overly impressed with the battlefield effectiveness of our infantry. The American soldier has no need of an apologist for, when well-disciplined, trained and led, he is second to none. We rightly refused to put flesh against steel. Because of our concept of the value and sanctity of human life, we employed masses of planes, artillery and armor to beat down resistance and enable the foot soldier to advance with minimum losses. . . .

The American soldier, being a "money player" did not exhibit the toughness, skill, and efficiency he would have otherwise developed under greater stress.

Our experience in Korea proved his capacity to "take it and come back fighting." Jack went on to say that more psychological and basic toughening and training are needed to lessen losses. Vietnam would have borne out his criticism. He would have delighted in the smaller, more sophisticated force in the Mideast conflict of the Gulf War. He made his points forcibly, supported by research and statistics. One can visualize Odysseus making similar comments before the walls of Troy, but he was a king and commanded respect by virtue of his political standing. Jack was never a politician. He never played the army game, by which some incompetent soldiers acquired overblown status and rank.

He had a long and respected tenure at Fort Knox, where he commanded the weapons department, but after General Ridgway told him on a visit there, that his, General Ridgway's, promotion list would be consigned to the wastebasket by then President Eisenhower because of personal animosity, Jack realized that his long military career was winding down. What a blow that must have been to one whose whole adult life was built on platoons, battalions, and armies of fighting men. Anything after Korea was an anticlimax. To a battle-hardened soldier, peacetime was a tremendous psychological and emotional letdown. Odysseus must have felt the same uselessness as he straggled home to Greece.

The army had a policy of slowly eliminating the experienced but aging officers. They were led quietly and gently out to pasture, even as the cavalry horses in their meadow at Front Royal. Jack's pasture was as a regular army adviser, first, to the New Jersey National Guard units, then, to those of New York State. A supreme irony was that the inept colonel from his pre-Pearl Harbor days was commander of the National Guard for the entire country. He had been relieved of duty before the Normandy invasion and was booted upstairs on the political home front.

Interestingly, this general wrote a glowing efficiency report on the officer he had so frequently reprimanded back at the prewar encampment. He was not the only incompetent whom Jack had to deal with during this assignment. He also had to inspect local Guard units who were commanded by some officers he had relieved of duty during battles and sent home. Needless to say, they did not welcome his inspections, which he refused to warn them about beforehand.

They made their discomfort and hatred known but, at the same time, tried to curry favor by invitations to dinner, shows in New York, and so on. With his usual disinclination to veer from his path of integrity, he gave poor marks to some of these units. Although their cries were probably loud and directed to high places, his efficiency reports and letters of approval continued to flow from his superiors in Albany and Washington.

On this National Guard assignment, Jack was once again back in the area where he was born and grew up. This was where he had played professional football, baseball, and later polo. It was where his horses had been stabled and where he rode in the horse shows at Madison Square Garden. It must have been a bitter-sweet homecoming. His parents were gone, his horses were long gone, too. The formerly rural setting was overgrown with developments and traffic. The wars had changed everything. The only horses he saw now were those of the New York City Police Department. Their stable was near his office, and he visited the beautiful bays as often as he could. This police department requisitioned bay horses as they came on the market from Western dealers. They were then trained by their partners for use in city traffic and crowd control. He must have ached to get back in the saddle, but the long rides and battle scars, emotional and physical, made such activity impossible.

During the next few years, as had happened at Fort Knox, many foreign officers, including those of former enemies, such as Germany, were sent to him for instruction and observation. He received enthusiastic letters of thanks for his help. These may have helped ease his increasing depression and sadness as the inevitable end of his active career approached. His marriage was no longer anything but a formality, as Circe's secrets and age were making her increasingly unstable. Instead of being able to rely on a wife's understanding and support with the impending change of his lifestyle, he spent much time, energy, and money on a string of psychiatrists, medications, and hospitalizations. In 1960, after many hurried trips home from his New York offices because of her constant suicide threats and attempts, he decided to resign from the army and take retirement. The letters, retirement gifts, farewell lunches, and parties were little recompense for the great wrench and realization that he was no longer needed for a command or for teaching in the career he loved.

While these upsetting events were taking place on the East Coast, 3,000 miles away, Penny was faced with some difficult decisions of her own. She was battling dark days of indecision, which she hated. She knew her marriage was only a facade and that some change had to be made. Her senile mother-in-law died after months of useless life-support measures, and her husband sank deeper into a morass of paranoia.

She had along-accumulated store of vacation time that she would lose if she did not take it, so in 1959, she decided to take the children on a trip back East to get away from a miserable routine, mounting bills, and the increasingly psychotic manifestations in her husband. It was obvious that these were having a severe effect on herself and the children. She was unaware, of course, of the changes taking place in Jack's life. She and the children went sightseeing and visiting friends and relatives as though all was well, but subconsciously she knew it was only an intermission before the final act in what had become a Greek drama.

After the long overland drive and back, she realized, on returning home, she should have packed their clothing and not returned. Of course, there were legal considerations to such a move. She was able to understand later that her return to her problems was inevitable and a better way to arrange for their future. As soon as she had sorted out her decision, she began to send out resumes to various agencies. She decided that she would have to put much distance between her and her verbally abusive husband who blamed her for all his troubles.

He did not correlate any of his failures to his delusions of grandeur and the dislocation of wartime service. He attempted many grandiose real-estate schemes, which his bankers told him could not be accomplished, and became increasingly morose as they did not come to fruition. He was a very competent lawyer but refused to take any cases unless they met his unrealistic aspirations. Although, after leaving the service, he had been offered several lucrative positions, he refused to work for anyone and turned them down.

This infuriated Penny, who was trying to support the family on a small salary and pay the bills, which he increasingly caused as he tried to make an appearance of professional competence. At this point, Penny realized that they would have to put many miles between herself and this unfortunate man or they would be tarred with a brush of bankruptcy and mental disease.

Realizing that she had not seen the Pacific Coast and would probably not be back in the foreseeable future, Penny loaded the children and the dog into the little station wagon and headed down the coast to California. Although she had little money, traveling was never a problem financially. The back of their car held a cooler, a box of groceries, and a hot plate on one side and a mattress on the other. One child could sleep there while the other put down the reclining front seat as did Penny. They had wonderful breakfasts along the scenic coast with the seals, and lunches and dinners at parks where grills were available. They walked down the cliffs to see the lumbering sea lions and tried to swim in the icy Oregon coast waters. They found this was too uncomfortable until they neared Los Angeles at Santa Monica.

A colleague at her clinic had arranged with her family in Los Angeles to make a lovely beach-front "cottage" available to Penny and the children. Her coworkers understood her problems and respected her for taking on the care of the orphaned children. They tried their best to help her in her dilemma. The doctors with whom she worked, in an unusual show of support for a nurse, also tried to smooth her way. If it had not been for so many friends and their support, the situation would have been impossible. There was no money for expensive amusement parks and food, but the ocean and the wonderful beaches offered free entertainment. Her hosts had huge citrus groves, and Penny was invited to help herself. It was a pleasant trip until her increasingly psychotic spouse decided to join them for the trip home.

Arriving back, she saw even more clearly that the time for her departure was running out. She told the children that their foster-father was ill and that if they stayed, they would all suffer the same fate. He precipitated the split when he told her that she had "ruined my life." He moved out to an apartment he could neither afford nor care for. Penny decided that California, where she had applied for work, was not far enough away. She answered an ad from a large teaching hospital in Baltimore and was hired by phone after the application was received. With some help from her friends, she packed a U-Haul trailer hitched to the wagon.

About three blocks from their house, the trailer developed a flat tire. It was hardly an auspicious beginning to a new life, but the decision had been made, and they were on their way, and the cross-country trip of 1959 was repeated. The children viewed it as another fun trip. They read road maps and chamber-of-commerce brochures. On some of the mountain passes, the little wagon went up in first gear, and it seemed like it might not get to the top. They did some sightseeing on the way. They ran out of gas in Yellowstone National Park because the gas gauge was not working and Penny could not afford to have it repaired. Since night was approaching, Penny prepared the children to sleep in the car, but a park worker drove a forty-mile round trip to bring them gas. He even followed them to the park to be sure they arrived safely. She had two hundred dollars in her pocket, all that was left after fifteen years of work, but the relief of making and sticking to her decision made everything seem possible. After arriving at her brother's home, near Washington, she awoke to find they had again run out of gas. Surely some benign Providence or guardian angel had watched as they traveled east.

A few dollars from her mother's estate enabled Penny to get a mortgage on a Baltimore row house. It was a very hot Labor Day when they moved into their tiny new home. A frightful Eastern thunderstorm blew up that afternoon, happily after she and the children had unloaded their U-Haul. Neither the children nor their pet dog had ever seen a thunderstorm. They were too surprised to be afraid. Penny quickly reassured them by a few elementary science facts. They never were so astonished or afraid again, and, of course, the dog took his cue from the human reactions.

They had all stood the trip and the transition well. They had no furniture except packing boxes, and a refrigerator that Penny had managed to buy on credit on the holiday. It was like a picnic, and it was so good to be in a stable situation without having to walk gingerly around a psychotic man. As a matter of fact, when her husband realized that she was really going to move three thousand miles away, he visited and acted more nearly normal than he had for a long time. He was quite repentant and had asked her to stay. Later she received a letter saying he had made a horrible mistake and asked her to return. She wrote back one word—no! It had taken much soul-searching to make the break, but a psychiatrist at her clinic told her she had nothing to be guilty about and "should be able to sleep nights."

School started at the same time Penny was to begin her new career. She was to teach nursing students in a pediatric emergency setting. It was hectic, but interesting, and she used all her ability mentally and physically to adjust to the frequent poisoned, malnourished babies and their parents. Baltimore was a city of contrasts. It had much history, but in seventeenth-century slums, her department was constantly busy. At home, the children kept fairly close watch on each other by way of tattling. Penny told them that if their transgressions were serious enough, she'd "hear about them," and if they weren't, they'd best be forgotten. She found being a single parent was not difficult. She was the final authority. There was no one for them to run to, to override her decisions or discipline. It was just a matter of making promises and keeping them, either for treats or punishment. She was too busy and tired to worry about their minor matters.

Her son assumed the man-of-the-house role, helping with repairs and maintenance. His sister, who liked housework from her own mother's training as a tiny child, helped with it for a double allowance. All in all, it was a comfortable situation when Penny received her first checks and was able to buy some furniture. Both children made friends easily and were not bothered by the change of lifestyle and schools. A cat and dog helped relax everyone, and the lack of funds for entertainment or gifts did not seem very pressing. A friend lived near the ocean. When the heat became oppressive, Penny drove 150 miles for a few days of swimming and change of scenery.

As had happened before, there was no one to relieve her in the clinic, so vacation time accumulated. Finally she was told she would have to take the time off or lose it. She made a fateful decision to drive north, through New York State and New England to the Canadian border. It was new territory for Penny as well as for the children, and she enjoyed the beautiful scenery and interesting places. To avoid extra expense, they visited some tourist attractions where children were admitted free but adults were charged. Penny sent the children into some of the historic places but waited for them outside. She did not mind that to some might it have seemed a deprivation, but she wanted the children to see and learn as much as possible. They were a long way from the little orphaned children who were afraid of the boat on their first trip.

Years later, her daughter asked her how they had seen and done so many things when they had so little money to spend. It was a very pleasant time without the presence of an irascible husband and the attendant background of tension and conflict.

Before they left Baltimore, Penny realized that since the children were not natural children, she would have to make legal preparations to safeguard them should they have any accidents or upon her death. She had a life insurance policy as part of her fringe benefits, and she wanted to clarify the situation. She found that although Maryland had been founded by Catholic nobility and marriage had to be a religious procedure, divorce was very simple.

She consulted a lawyer, called a master in chancery, substantiated by a witness that she had been separated from her husband for over two years, and a divorce was granted. Her husband was notified at the Veterans Hospital, where he was a psychiatric patient. He made no objection. It was a great relief, but more important, she did not know that in New York, at that time, a divorce could not be obtained from a psychiatric patient. Again some benevolent force was guiding her life as had so often happened before.

After several weeks of traveling through the northeast from the Maine coast through Cape Cod and on down the busy cities, they headed south, on their way back to Baltimore. All through the years, Penny had given up even thinking and dreaming of what might have been. The war had brought Jack to her and had taken him away. There was no use reliving what could not be helped. As they drove down the crowded interstate, Penny had a strange feeling. The past came over her with a rush.

She stopped at a roadside rest area, telling the children she wanted to look up an address. She knew she was in the general area where Jack had lived. She felt as though some irresistible force was guiding her to the bulky telephone directory. Sure enough, under the county listing, was Jack's name and title. He was home!

She made a note of his address, not far from where she had the premonition. She knew she had to make a digression to see how and where he was living. She seemed to have no volition in this decision. It was as though a magnet was drawing her to this man she had loved so hopelessly. After twenty long years, the feelings, so long denied, were still there.

The address was in a suburban development of newer homes on winding streets. It was some time before she could locate the proper street. She asked directions in a haze and finally found the curving drive. Her heart was beating so hard, she had trouble concealing her nervousness from the children, who were in the backseat. As she approached the house, she could see Jack outside, fussing about with a car. If he had not been outside the house, she would have driven on by and continued on her way home. But there he was, twenty years older, but still the man she had apparently continued loving unconsciously and thought she had irretrievably lost.

She adjusted her sunglasses and parked across the street. She lightly tapped the horn. He looked up and came toward them. As he approached, she lowered her sunglasses. He stopped as though struck by lightning. It was really a tremendous moment in both their lives. They just looked at each other, unable to speak. Then Penny introduced the children, mentioning that they were her foster children. Somehow, she did not want him to think they were the offspring of another man. They exchanged very few words, but the electricity was still there. She told him where she was living, and he told her he had retired. He did not mention Circe or his circumstances, and she, of course, did not ask. In all, she was only there for about five minutes. The tension was too great to be borne longer.

She put the car in gear and explained to the children that this was someone she had known before they were born. She drove slowly away. She knew instinctively that Odysseus was back in her life, but how and when they would meet again was in the lap of whatever gods there might be.

It was a very hot day along the Jersey shore, so with her usual love of the sea, they stopped several times for reviving swims and fast food. That night, they camped near the Delaware River. In the morning, they boarded the ferry and were soon home in Baltimore. It had been an unexpected and disturbing climax to their trip. The children accepted her explanation of "an old friend," but Penny knew that it was so much more than that. How and when it would end, she had no idea, but so much of her life had been coincidence or fate or whatever, she was prepared to wait and see what would happen. It was obvious that he was married. Knowing his basic integrity, although her acceptance of that was seriously strained, it was difficult to look ahead.

Penny now was faced with the knowledge that she was irretrievably still in love with a man she had tried to forget for twenty years. She waited for a call from him, but none came. He did not have her address, although with his background in intelligence operations, he could surely have found her. She decided to play a more active role in their future.

She had many pictures taken while he was still with his beloved horses. She had taken dozens to get their heads in a good pose. There were also some of his old friends in the regiment, many of whom were long gone or scattered. She placed one or two in a blank sheet of paper in an envelope with no name but with her return address. They were mailed several times a year. She received no answer. She was devastated but, characteristically, did not have time or energy to again grieve for what she felt was another loss and rejection.

Later he was to tell her that he wanted to call, to see her again, but his wife was so psychotic and incapacitated that, if he had communicated, he would have abandoned Circe, and that he could not bring himself to do. He apparently did not think that it would have been so hard on Penny, but he was never a student of female behavior and sensitivity, although he was always aware of the emotions and needs of his troops. Penny felt badly abused and eventually gave up the attempt to rekindle their love.

Penny had registered for college courses to achieve a graduate degree as soon as she had been accepted to a new position. She was keenly aware that she needed every possible credential to support herself and the children. The hospital paid her tuition as long as she maintained a B average. School had never been a problem for her. It was good for the children to realize that adults needed to go to school, too. She took her son with her to the night classes for protection and to keep him on a bit of a leash, as he was tall and looked much older than he was. Occasionally, as they walked to her car, parked some distance off campus, there were suspicious rustlings and movement in the shrubbery. Robberies and muggings were not uncommon on campus, but she felt the tall boy would discourage those possibilities. It apparently worked, for in the three years that she had spent in night school, they were never harmed.

Penny was able to complete the degree requirements in three years. This would qualify her for a college teaching position at a better salary and hours than the hospital could afford. She was also more interested in teaching community-based students the elements of public health and prevention. The inbred values the hospital placed on cure and research were in direct conflict with her conception of prevention rather than the preoccupation with those whose lifestyles assured that they would be candidates for the surgeon's knife or the life-support systems so dear to the heart of technology-oriented doctors.

During these years, although she felt slighted and rejected, she continued in a demanding job, with growing children and their special needs, and trips to the mountains and the seashore and family gatherings. If Jack had communicated with her, it would have been easier to bear, but Plato's "born soldiers" didn't communicate easily. She should have thought back to the World War II V-mail letters which had stopped when he and his soldiers readied for the assault on Normandy. She also never knew the reasons for that lapse for years.

No longer considering the possibility of Jack's return to her, Penny settled for a position at a college far out on Long Island. It was another dislocation for the teenaged children, but that was solved by bringing along several of their Baltimore friends for a few weeks of visiting. By the time their friends returned to their own homes, both children had made new friends. Again, they adjusted well to a more rural setting near the ocean. A psychological evaluation while they were still in Baltimore revealed that they hardly remembered their own parents and considered Penny their real mother.

Their brand-new home was pleasant and large enough for some degree of privacy. Their Baltimore row house had been so small that Penny had given the bedroom to the children and slept in the living room. The setting was much more enjoyable with a golf course on three sides and the beaches only a few miles away. They had lost their pet dog before the move but found a new beagle and a stray cat who adopted them. The children began to socialize with their schoolmates but seemed worried about Penny. They called her when they were out in the evening to make sure she was all right. They seemed to worry that she did not have a social life and probably unconsciously felt she was grieving for that old friend.

She felt no interest in promoting any interest in any of her contacts as far as dates were concerned. She was fortunate that her colleagues were congenial. Her students were more mature, and their progress toward a career more fulfilling than the hospital students who were less able to relate to their patients. She was glad that her days were so full and pleasant. Her West Coast years seemed far away and best forgotten, although she frequently heard from her former husband's family, who had always been thankful for her efforts on behalf of their relative. They never blamed her for his problems, which they once told her had existed before his service and her involvement.

Life went on uneventfully for several years. Penny wrote a manual for students, which was published by a major firm. It freed her from daily assignments, which were covered in the book the students could buy. Writing was once described as an excuse for living. For her it seemed a release from frustration and tension, which she never voiced.

As the third holiday season approached, Penny became very unhappy. She had ceased sending out the pictures some time ago. It had been so unproductive that she felt it was surely all over and a waste of time to even think about. She decided that she would not attend the inevitable parties that the faculty and students always held. It was too painful to wander in without an escort or even a friend. She knew the children would be upset, as they planned for their own festivities, but if her life could not include Jack, she did not want to open it to anyone else.

Just as Penny made this decision, on a Saturday morning, several weeks before Christmas, her phone rang. She picked it up. The well-remembered voice caused her to sit down heavily. It was so unexpected. She could hardly respond. He told her that Circe had died ten days before. Now he wanted to see her. Could he come? Penny was uncertain. How could she forgive the long silent years? Could those years ever be bridged? Without conscious thought, she gave him directions and hung up the phone.

What could she say when they finally met on her own turf? What would they look like to each other after so many years? Her indecision was so great that she was unable to eat and lost a great deal of weight in one week. As he drove up, he was not the tattered Odysseus of Homer's tale but a tired shadow of his former healthy self. There didn't seem to be any need for words. Odysseus was home!